DATAFILES

Science now

Sarah Angliss

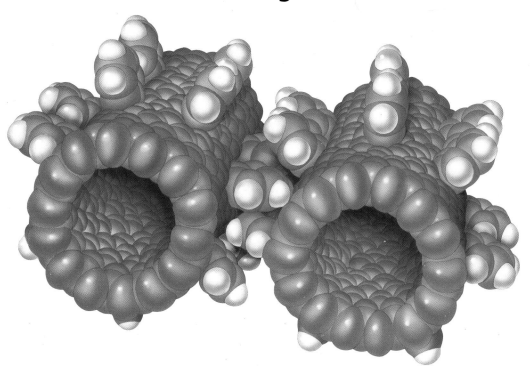

Silver Dolphin

Contents

Published in the United States by
Silver Dolphin Books
An imprint of the Advantage Publishers Group
5880 Oberlin Drive, San Diego, CA 92121-4794
www.advantagebooksonline.com

A Marshall Edition
Conceived, edited, and designed by
Marshall Editions Ltd
The Orangery
161 New Bond Street
London W1S 2UF
www.marshallpublishing.com

ISBN 1-57145-481-0
Library of Congress Cataloging-in-Publication Data available
upon request.

Originated in Singapore by Master Image
Printed and bound in China by Excel Printing

1 2 3 4 5   00 01 02 03 04

Cover photography: front, tl Photodisc, tr Honda,
cl K.H. Kjeldsen/Science Photo Library, cr Donna Caveney/MIT,
bl David Parker for ESA/CNES/Ariane Space/Science Photo Library,
br Mark Joseph/gettyone Stone; back, Overview, In Focus: Digital
Vision, Storyfile: Alfred Pasieka/Science Photo Library, FAQs:
Digital Vision, Jobfile: Michael Roberts, Factfile: Digital Vision.

FAQs

FACTFILE

JOBFILE

How this book works

OVERVIEW

This colorful opening section introduces the amazing world of science. Alongside a spectacular montage of images that gives us a flavor of science and technology, this mini-essay looks at how science is part of all our lives. It explains how humans have always been curious about the world around them, and how this has led to scientific discoveries and inventions.

FAQs

Packed full of fascinating facts, the FAQs—Frequently Asked Questions—file provides answers to some of the questions you've always wanted to ask. How did space and time begin? Can we make designer babies? Are machines smarter than humans? Are we alone in the universe? And many other fascinating questions.

JOBFILE

This file shows you what it's like to be a scientist. There are interviews with people about their careers in science, including how they got started and what their job involves. Although the people are fictional, the work they describe is based on real life.

IN FOCUS

This section focuses on the essential information about today's scientific knowledge. Beautifully illustrated with photographs and diagrams, the section looks at computers, robots, genetics, medicine, atoms, energy, nanotechnology, materials, and many other fascinating subjects.

FACTFILE

Providing ready reference at a glance, this file contains essential facts and figures in an easy-to-access format. It includes facts about atoms, powers of ten, useful plants, as well as timelines and a comprehensive illustrated glossary that explains technical terms used in the book.

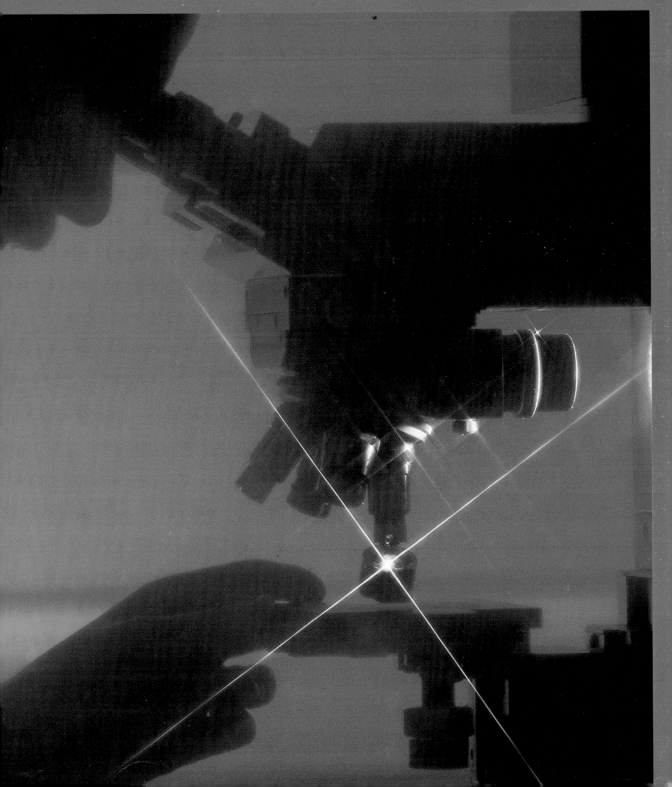

Overview

Natural scientists

5–8

"Today, our machines are still simple creations, hardly worthy of the word 'intelligent.' But within the next century they will mature into entities as complex as ourselves."

Hans Moravec, robotics researcher at Carnegie Mellon University, U.S.,
writing on the future of thinking machines, 1988

Perhaps you don't think of yourself as a scientist. Maybe for you, science is something that's performed by people in white coats in remote laboratories. But that would be underestimating the scope of science—and your own, breathtaking abilities. You are human, so you are a scientist.

Over the centuries, science has developed along with language, crafts, and every other element of human understanding and culture. Piecing together the fragments left behind by early

humans, archaeologists have revealed the findings of the very first scientists. Observing how hot flames could melt iron from stone, for example, our ancestors learned to use metals around 8,000 years ago. Just like 21st-century technologists, their imaginations soared with this new discovery. These early humans devised countless uses and experiments for metals, laying the foundations of many branches of science and engineering still in use today.

"You are human, so you are a scientist."

Science has helped other areas of human culture to flourish in countless ways. The first people to learn the science of sowing and harvesting wheat, for example, lived in the Middle East around 12,000 years ago. Their discoveries enabled people to stockpile food for the first time, instead of finding it from day to day. With food in storage, people could settle in one place,

building new communities and cities. By the beginning of the first millennium, wheat had enabled many cities to flourish across Europe and Asia. The first wheat growers were our earliest biotechnologists, people who learned to change plants or plant habitats in some way. Some of today's biotechnologists can directly alter the inherited traits of plants. Others search through the plants already in existence, looking for sources of powerful new medicines. It's fascinating to imagine the changes that their discoveries will bring.

Humans can't help being good at science. Just watch a toddler trying to climb onto a chair to see what's out of reach on the table above him or her. Even as children, we are naturally curious—and science is just an expression of our curiosity. However, the curiosity of scientists goes far beyond the immediate world around them. Scientists try to discover what's out of reach in distant galaxies, the core of the planet, the inner world of the atom, the genes within our

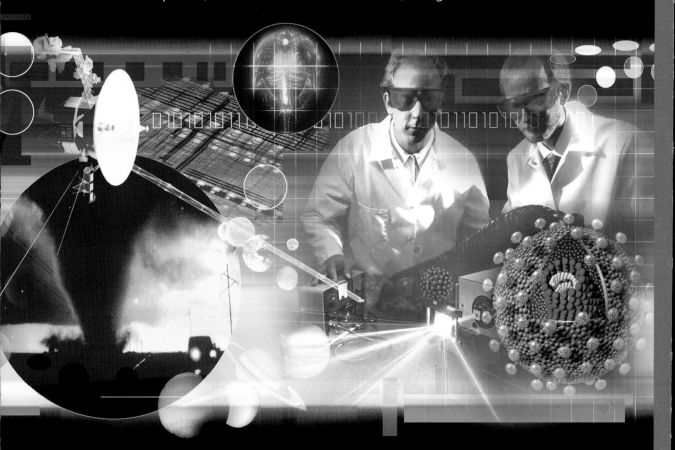

cells, the past and the future. They must use the highest standards of investigation because new ideas and discoveries are usually only accepted when there is adequate evidence to support them. This is the very essence of modern science.

A baby may rely on its eyes, ears, nose, fingers, or mouth to test the world around it. But scientists and engineers have developed a wide variety of machines to

"Scientists try to discover what's out of reach."

extend the sensing abilities of the body. Microscopes, scanners, telescopes, and other imaging technology all enable us to glimpse the unreachable. They show us worlds that would otherwise be too tiny, too distant, or too dangerous to be within our grasp.

The word science comes from *scientia*—the Latin for "knowledge." Knowing and understanding what makes up living things, materials, the Earth, and the universe is part of what modern

science is about. But some of the most exciting areas of science and technology are those we are only just beginning to understand. If you've ever been curious to know why your body will eventually age and die, or if there's other life in the universe, or how long the Earth will survive, then you are not alone. Scientists have never stopped wondering about questions such as these. If you'd like to know more about how they are searching for answers and what treasures have sprung from their discoveries, then read on...

IN FOCUS

In Focus

The information age

Neural nets • IT • Supercomputer • Wearable computers

We are living through a scientific revolution, made possible by computers. These machines allow every one of us, including scientists, to access information and perform calculations faster than was ever before possible.

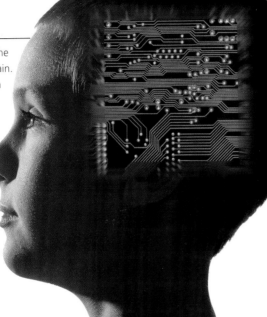

△ **Supercomputers are used by scientists for research to improve weather forecasting.**

Thinking power

A computer has only a fraction of the "thinking power" of the human brain. A typical computer has a few billion tiny memory units, each connected to only one or two others. Your brain has 100 billion cells, called neurons, which form a complex web of connections. Scientists have made electronic versions of neurons. These "neural networks" can learn and adapt to changing situations, just like a living mind.

▷ **The brain has a far more complex network of connections than a computer chip.**

Research tools

Supercomputers can carry out huge calculations faster than any machine ever built. Scientists use them to do sums that would be practically impossible by hand. With supercomputers, meteorologists (weather scientists) can put together thousands of rainfall, wind, and air temperature measurements to forecast the weather.

Virtual trips

Most of us rely on a screen, keyboard, and mouse when we communicate with computers. In the future, we may have more user-friendly alternatives to these "interfaces." The VR helmet and dataglove are interfaces that allow you to interact with a computer using head and hand movements. You see a scene in the helmet which shifts, just like real life, when you turn your head. Move your gloved hand, and the computer moves a picture of your hand in the scene.

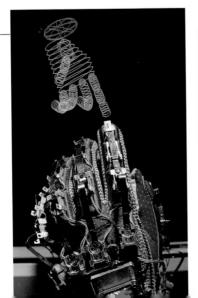

Wearing computers

In the future, computers may be built into clothes and glasses. Designers are already experimenting with wearable computers. Voice-activated computers embedded in coveralls, for example, could be used by paramedics who need to keep their hands free. Tiny projectors mounted on glasses could beam medical information into their eyes.

◁ **Tiny pockets all over this dataglove (left) fill with air, squeezing your hand. This makes you feel that you are grasping real objects.**

SEE ALSO

Thinking machines	10–11
Are any machines smarter than humans?	42–43
Thinking power	70–71

Thinking machines

Smart robots • Machine sensing • Insect robots
Remote robots • Turing Test • Intelligent car

They smile, teach each other things and dodge chairs around the laboratory—the latest robots under development really can think for themselves. A few are already being put to work replacing human brainpower with their artificial intelligence.

Just a machine?

Whether they're smelling perfumes or finding faulty goods on a production line, robots with artificial intelligence can already do many jobs without human control. Scientists think that machines that act like humans may be easier to use. Kismet (right) was designed by researchers trying to mimic human behavior with machines. He looks sad if you ignore him! A robot gets its thinking power from advanced computers. But as scientists develop more intelligent systems, they raise more questions about the mind—the source of human thinking power. Does a robot that can make a decision like a person have a mind? Or is it just another machine?

Seeing robots

Researchers are only just beginning to build robots that can see as well as living creatures. Seeing is about much more than simply picking up images of a scene. Lots of thinking power is needed to make sense of these images. A seeing robot needs to recognize and track particular objects as it moves.

▽ **A tiny, antlike robot sits on a researcher's hand.**

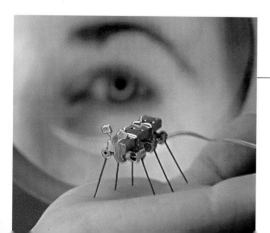

◁ **A sensing robot with a model of the insect that inspired it.**

Insect robots

Designing a machine that is as skilled as a human is a very ambitious task. It's not surprising that many researchers stick to something a little easier. Insect robots are a popular choice. Researchers are currently trying to make insect robots that can teach each other things. However, even the simplest robot needs a giant computer to give it the intelligence of an ant.

Life-savers

Thinking machines can save lives when they work in places that are too risky for people to go. Astronauts, divers, bomb disposal experts, and other people working in dangerous places have used robots for many years. Until recently, their machines had no "thinking power." Experts had to watch them from a place of safety and work them by remote control. Now, many robots have on-board intelligence so they can work on their own. A team of bomb disposal robots, for example, can see objects around them and work together to deal with explosives. These robots can do almost as much as the human experts.

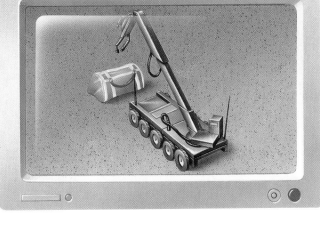

▷ **An intelligent robot looks for a bomb in a sealed-off city street.**

◁ **Kismet was designed by researchers trying to mimic human behavior with machines. Here he is looking happy.**

Computer test

The ultimate test of computer intelligence was devised by a computer pioneer during World War II. Realizing that it may one day be possible to make very powerful computers, the British mathematician Alan Turing wondered how he could tell if they were truly "intelligent." He suggested a computer intelligence test that was simple to run, but extremely difficult to pass (see pages 42–43). No computer comes close to passing it, even today. The best ones can only pass the test if it is confined to a limited range of subjects. A medical computer, for example, may seem smart if asked about digestion—but hopeless if questioned about vacations!

SEE ALSO

Are any machines smarter than humans?	42–43
Thinking power	70–71
Glossary	78–81

Taking the wheel

The engines and transmissions of many of the latest cars are worked by computer. Some computers can even control the distance from the car ahead. However, it will be many more years before a computer can take over completely from the driver. Car driving is one of the most complex practical jobs a human does, and it takes hundreds of hours of practice to become expert at driving on busy roads. A driver's brain has to respond in a split second to lots of changing information. No computer designed so far is as good as a human at this task.

△ **We are unlikely to see a completely driverless car in the near future.**

Breaking the code

Reading the past • Double helix • Characteristics • Recreating dinosaurs Artificial reproduction • Natural selection

Inside every one of your body's cells is a chemical called deoxyribonucleic acid—or DNA for short—which helps to make you who you are. Scientists are learning how to read and use the code that is carried by DNA.

▽ **A parent and child will usually look similar because they share half of their DNA.**

Skin color is passed on through genes

Girl has inherited her mother's artistic skills

Boy is athletic, unlike his father

You are unique

The science of DNA, called genetics, may help us to understand a lot more about ourselves. The DNA in a living thing acts like its blueprint, helping to control how it lives, grows, and develops. Only if you are an identical twin will you have the same DNA as another person. Scientists are trying to discover how DNA works inside the body, how it evolved, and how it copies itself from cell to cell. They are interested not only in the DNA of living things. Comparing tiny traces of DNA from ancient corpses or from fossils gives them clues about links with living creatures. This research may help scientists to discover more about human history or extinct animals.

▷ **Buried and preserved in peat for centuries, this ancient body may give up more of its secrets if scientists can read some of its DNA.**

DNA double helix

Atom spiral

DNA is made of a long chain of atoms joined together in a twisting shape called a double helix. The British and American scientists James Watson and Francis Crick worked out the shape of DNA in 1953. Their breakthrough was based on earlier research made by French scientist Rosalind Franklin, who showed that the atoms in DNA form a spiraling structure.

△ **Scientists aren't sure of the influence of DNA on many characteristics, such as being artistic or good at sports. Are these skills entirely due to the way people are brought up?**

Just like your parents?

You are probably like other members of your natural family. This is partly due to DNA. Half of your DNA was copied from your mother and half from your father. Your mother and father, in turn, have copies of DNA from your grandparents. Characteristics such as eye and natural hair color are always inherited. They are passed on very simply by DNA. The causes of some other characteristics are much harder to unravel. Height is an example. Is your adult height completely controlled by your DNA—or does diet and level of exercise also play a part?

What helped this girl to become a good violinist?

▷ **Darwin studied the varied shells of the giant turtles on Galápagos to develop his theory of natural selection. Genetic scientists study the DNA of these creatures today.**

Dinosaur DNA

Science fiction writers have written about recreating dinosaurs, early humans, and other extinct animals using DNA from their remains. But in the real world, the DNA in dead bodies gradually decays. There will never be enough DNA in these ancient fossils to bring extinct creatures back to life. However, traces of DNA left in fossilized bones may help scientists to learn more about evolution.

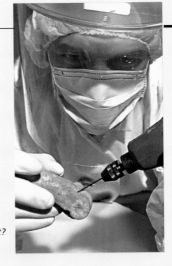

◁ **These bone samples from a Neanderthal man may contain fragments of ancient DNA.**

Gift of life

All of us received our DNA from our natural parents. A father's DNA is carried in his sperm, a mother's in her eggs. A few of us had our parents' DNA brought together in a laboratory. In a procedure called in vitro fertilization (IVF), sperm from a father fertilizes an egg from a mother in a dish, making a cell that could develop into a new baby.

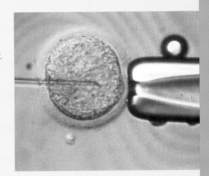

▷ **A father's sperm is injected directly into a mother's egg. This procedure can help couples who have problems conceiving children.**

Galápagos discoveries

In the 19th century, the British scientist Charles Darwin made some important discoveries about inheritance. His inspiration came from the Galápagos Islands in the Pacific Ocean. Darwin found that the traits (characteristics) of animals living on the Galápagos varied slightly from island to island, matching differences in the animals' surroundings. If the only insects lived deep under the sand, for example, birds on that island had long beaks. Darwin realized that traits which helped survival became stronger from generation to generation. This effect, called natural selection, could explain how all animals evolved to survive in their habitats.

SEE ALSO

The new genetics

Resistant crops • Xenotransplants • GMOs
Cloning the sheep • Genetic engineering • Mixing species

As scientists unlock the secrets of DNA, they are also learning how to change the genetic code itself. In a new branch of science, called genetic engineering, scientists have learned how to change plants and animals, and even to create new forms of life.

On the farm

Around the world, some farmers are already putting genetic engineering to work. They are growing crops that have artificially altered DNA. Some of these crops are resistant to weedkillers; others make chemicals that poison insect pests. A few are living "factories"—some, for example, make the raw ingredients for new medicines.

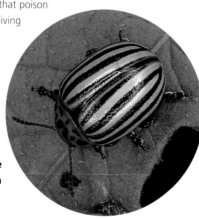

▷ **Poisons in a genetically altered potato plant kill the stripy Colorado beetle (right), a pest that can destroy potato crops.**

New organs

A person who needs a new organ relies on a transplant from a human donor. But there are not enough donated human organs to go around. Animal organs are genetically different from human ones, so they can't be used. However, scientists are putting fragments of human DNA into animals so they will grow into organs that people can use, called xenotransplants.

◁ **Patients waiting for kidneys from human donors have to undergo regular dialysis (left) to purify their blood. Xenotransplants, from animals with some human genes, may give them an alternative source of hope.**

Genetically modified food

Genetically modified (altered) food is already available in the supermarkets—but many people are still weighing its possible benefits and risks. Makers of genetically altered plants, or GMOs, claim that they reduce the need for weedkillers and produce more plentiful crops. Critics are concerned that these crops may pass their unusual DNA to other plants around them, especially to related wild plants.

Genetically modified soy in instant food

Rice

Grapes

Corn on the cob

Shopper's jacket contains genetically modified cotton

Tomatoes genetically modified to increase their shelf life

Hello Dolly

A sheep code-named Dolly made the headlines in 1997 when her breeders announced that she was a clone. A clone has all its DNA taken from the cell of another creature—it's a perfect genetic duplicate. Dolly was the first mammal ever to be cloned from an ordinary adult cell. Earlier mammal clones took their DNA from eggs. It wasn't easy to make Dolly—she was the only one of 250 attempted sheep clones that survived until birth. Scientists have strong motives to make cloning more reliable. A herd of sheep clones, for example, could be genetically modified to make medicines in their milk.

Nonreproductive cell

Cells cultured to produce a crop

DNA taken from best cell

Dolly

Egg

DNA removed from egg

DNA fused with egg

Egg with DNA develops to form Dolly

△ **How Dolly the cloned sheep was produced from two other ewes.**

▽ **Genetically modified substances are used in some, but not all, products.**

Soy in this bread was modified to make it resistant to insect pests

Apples

Bananas

Meat from livestock fed on genetically modified food

Fish (salmon)

Carrots

Genetically modified bacteria clotted this hard cheese

Distant relatives

People tried to change the traits of living things centuries before the discovery of DNA. Today, we'd call their activities genetic engineering. The domestic dog is a good example. Over thousands of years, pet dogs have been developed from wolves. Early humans who wanted wolves to share their homes probably selected ones that were relatively small and gentle. Over many generations they chose wolves with these particular characteristics for breeding, ending up with an animal much smaller and gentler than its wolf ancestors—something very like the modern dog.

▷ **It's easy to forget that the wolf (far right) and the dachsund (right) are distant cousins.**

Chimaeras and hybrids

Scientists can already mix whole cells of different animals to create new creatures called chimeras. In 1984, they mixed cells from a sheep and goat to make a chimera called a geep. Creatures made by splicing the DNA from one species into another are called "hybrids." They can be used in many areas of research. A creature made by splicing fragments of mammoth DNA into elephant, for example, could bring us closer to these extinct elephant ancestors.

△ **This geep (half goat, half sheep) was made by mixing together the cells from two different species.**

SEE ALSO

Can we make designer babies?	40–41
Genetics breakthroughs	74–75
Glossary	78–81

Spare parts

Organ transplants • Nervous system • Hip joints
Tissue factories • Artificial blood • Coral implants

New developments in the science of materials are being coupled with advances in growing living body material to make a wide range of replacement parts for the body, including working human organs. Artificial body parts such as these could allow many of us to live longer, more active lives.

▽ **Early experiments in building bridges for broken bones have been very successful. The bridge is made of a plastic scaffolding (1). Bone is transplanted onto the scaffolding and grows over it (2). Once the bone has completely covered it, the scaffolding dissolves away (3).**

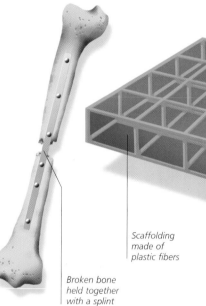

Scaffolding made of plastic fibers

Broken bone held together with a splint

Replacement organs

The list of patients waiting for donated organs is always very long. Organs such as hearts and livers come from people who have given their bodies to medicine after death. Even when an organ is available, a transplant carries many risks. It's not surprising that doctors are trying to find other replacements for failing organs. Some scientists are experimenting with artificial organs that contain living body cells.

△ ▷ **A transplant team races to deliver a donated liver to a patient.**

Walking again

Electronics could one day be used to help paralyzed accident victims. Wires can replace parts of the damaged nervous system that should connect the legs to the brain. A computer linked to these wires sends tiny electrical pulses along them, just like the pulses made by living nerves. If the pulses are sent in the right order, they could enable the user to walk again.

Wear and tear

Many people are very active until their old age, so their joints suffer lots of wear and tear. If a person's hip joint becomes worn, he or she can find it painful to move around. Fortunately, the worn-out joint can be swapped for an artificial replacement. This has a metal stem, connected to the thighbone, and a metal socket, connected to the pelvis. These two parts are cemented onto the bone that surrounds them. The socket of an artificial hip is lined with a smooth, tough plastic so the hip can move without wearing away.

▷ **This hip joint is made from materials that are tough enough to last 20 years.**

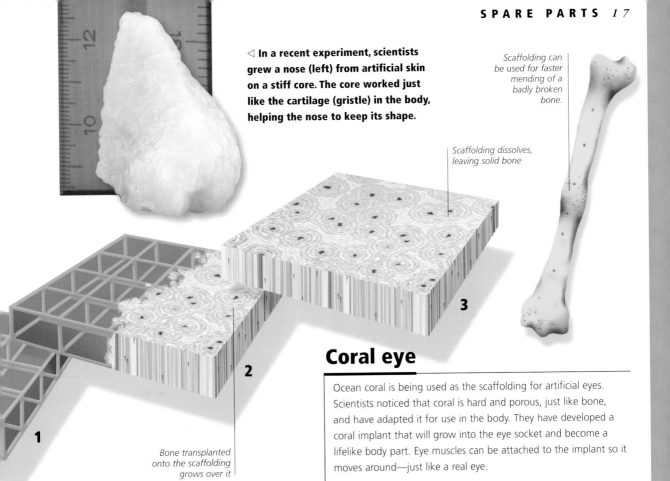

◁ **In a recent experiment, scientists grew a nose (left) from artificial skin on a stiff core. The core worked just like the cartilage (gristle) in the body, helping the nose to keep its shape.**

Scaffolding can be used for faster mending of a badly broken bone.

Scaffolding dissolves, leaving solid bone

Bone transplanted onto the scaffolding grows over it

1
2
3

Coral eye

Ocean coral is being used as the scaffolding for artificial eyes. Scientists noticed that coral is hard and porous, just like bone, and have adapted it for use in the body. They have developed a coral implant that will grow into the eye socket and become a lifelike body part. Eye muscles can be attached to the implant so it moves around—just like a real eye.

△ **Coral from the seabed forms the basis for a realistic artificial eye.**

Tissue factories

Scientists have tried to make artificial organ parts for many years. A plastic heart valve, for example, can replace a real valve that has failed inside a body. (A valve is a body part that stops blood from flowing the wrong way.) Scientists can even make machines that do the work of entire organs. The "kidney machine," used outside the body, already works well. It keeps patients with kidney problems alive by dialysis while they wait for kidney transplants (see page 14). Other organs, such as the liver, are much harder to replace with machines. That's why scientists are experimenting with machines incorporating living human cells. They hope to make an artificial liver, for example, that has real liver cells. The cells would clean the blood in a way that no machine can.

New blood

One day, we may be able to replace donated blood with blood made in the laboratory. At present, all the blood used in hospitals comes from human donors. But some people have rare blood types for which it is hard to find supplies, and there's always a risk that donated blood will pass on disease. These problems could be solved with artificial blood. Researchers have already developed artificial blood cells that can survive long enough to carry gases or drugs into the body.

▷ **This blood was donated by a human, but one day blood could be made artificially.**

Beating disease

Infectious diseases • Germs and viruses • John Snow
Melting icecaps • Epidemiologists

Although medicine can fight many diseases, researchers are still looking for ways to tackle some of the most ancient killers, including malaria, Asian influenza, and cancer. They are also searching for new ways to understand and combat human disease.

Working with killers

Heart disease, cancer, and many other big killers can't be spread from person to person. Even the most dangerous infectious diseases, such as the HIV virus and the plague, offer few risks to people researching them. But a few deadly diseases can be spread so easily that scientists have to work with them in special sealed booths. These include infections such as Ebola and Lassa fever—killers that can be spread from one person to another through the air. Thankfully, these diseases are extremely rare.

Fighting infections

Germs and viruses breed so fast that they can evolve into new strains (types) within days. Most of them develop this way when there are changes in their surroundings. Some germs, for example, respond to the antibiotics that doctors prescribe to overcome them. Gradually, the germs form new strains that are resistant to these drugs. Doctors try to limit the prescription of antibiotics so these medicines remain effective in the fight against germs. Meanwhile, researchers are trying to develop new drugs that can evolve as fast as germs.

◁ *Staphylococcus aureus* germs, viewed under the microscope here, are the common causes of boils, abscesses, and other treatable infections. A few, rare strains of this germ are resistant to almost all antibiotics.

◁ In 1997 a deadly strain of avian (bird) flu broke out in Hong Kong. The virus that caused this infection jumped from birds to humans, with devastating results.

▽ A scientist inspects some deadly germs that have been cultured (grown) inside this sealed booth. Air inside the booth is filtered to make sure no harmful organisms can escape.

Removing the source

Some diseases can be tackled without fully understanding their cause—or how they are triggered in the body. Researchers who deal with diseases in this way are called epidemiologists. They try to beat disease by looking at the people who suffer from them and the lifestyles that they have in common. Epidemiologists studying cancer, for example, have found that lung cancer is very common among heavy smokers. One of the most celebrated early epidemiologists was a British doctor called John Snow. Working in London around 150 years ago, he managed to combat an outbreak of cholera without any knowledge of the germ that caused it. We now know cholera is a deadly disease that is passed on through germs found in sewage. During a cholera outbreak in 1854, Snow interviewed people in the streets affected by the disease. He found that all the cholera sufferers took water from a pump that had an inlet downstream of a sewer pump. When Snow removed the pump, the cholera outbreak rapidly went away.

△ A water pump in London, similar to the one found by John Snow to be the source of the 1854 cholera outbreak.

SEE ALSO

Can we make designer babies?	40–41
Why can't science help us live for ever?	44–45
Plants that cure	72–73

Looking for clues

▽ Germs and viruses that caused diseases in the distant past could be frozen in the Earth's icecaps. Would any ancient diseases return if the icecaps melted?

Over the last 100 years, the lifestyles of people in industrialized countries have changed faster than ever before. In general, we eat more and exercise less than our ancestors. Unlike them, we're exposed every day to car fumes, pesticides, and electric fields from our TVs, radios, and cellular phones. There is no doubt that some of these changes have had an impact on human health. Many epidemiologists gather data about lifestyles and disease to research the effects of modern living.

▽ Recent research has shown no link between cellular phones and cancers.

The big thaw

If global warming is happening (see pages 32–33), it could lead to new outbreaks of disease. A warmer world would have tropical temperatures in more northerly areas, such as northern Europe. Tropical diseases such as malaria and yellow fever could become widespread in these places. A few scientists have suggested that the North and South poles could also be sources of disease in a warmer world. They fear that many disease-causing germs and viruses could be frozen into the icecaps at the poles. If the climate becomes much warmer, much of the ice could melt, releasing ancient germs and viruses into the atmosphere.

Inside the atom

Quarks • Particle accelerators
Gluons • Matter and antimatter

To search for answers about some of the smallest particles that can exist, scientists are carrying out huge experiments. In giant machines, known as particle accelerators, scientists make these tiny particles move at almost the speed of light. They crash the particles into each other or against solid targets, then search through the debris of the collisions. They hope these experiments will give them clues about the basic building blocks of the universe.

△ **The CERN rings have been drawn on this photograph.**

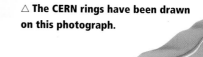

Offices above ground

Particles traveling counterclockwise

Electrons

◁ **A typical atom is made up of a cloud of lightweight particles, called electrons, that flit randomly around a cluster of much heavier particles, called protons and neutrons.**

Protons and neutrons form the nucleus

Colliding particles

Atoms, the tiny particles that make up every solid, liquid, and gas, are themselves made up of even smaller particles: protons, neutrons, and electrons. At places such as CERN in Geneva, Switzerland, and SLAC in Stanford, C.A., scientists are trying to smash some of these subatomic particles apart, revealing their ingredients. At present, they do not think the electron is made of smaller particles. But there is evidence that a cluster of three smaller particles makes up each proton and neutron. Scientists call these mystery particles quarks. According to their latest theories, all matter in the universe, from a drop of water to a star, is made entirely from quarks and lightweight particles, including electrons. However, no one has yet discovered how to capture a quark and store it on its own.

◁ **Engineers in front of a machine that is used to detect particles in a CERN accelerator. Scientists pump air out of the accelerator so there is nothing to slow down the particles under test. They do this so thoroughly that they make the accelerator more empty than outer space.**

Big science

Particle accelerators are far too massive to fit in a laboratory. The largest CERN accelerator is ring-shaped, but SLAC's main accelerator is a long, straight tube. Both of them are huge—the CERN ring is over 16 miles in circumference.

A team of scientists from around 20 different countries work together at CERN, performing experiments that can take several months to prepare. Huge bursts of electricity are used to push particles, stripped from individual atoms, around the accelerator. Strong magnets stop the fast-moving particles from veering off course.

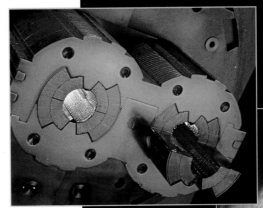

◁ The strong magnets inside this new particle accelerator at CERN are made of superconductors (see pages 80–81).

▷ A view inside the ring-shaped accelerator at CERN, called the LEP collider (LEP stands for large electron positron—see below).

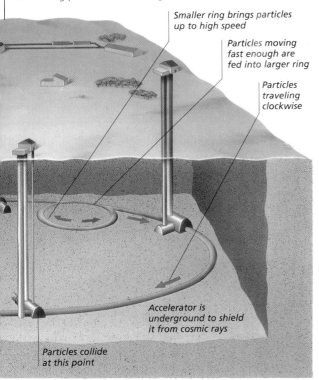

Smaller ring brings particles up to high speed

Particles moving fast enough are fed into larger ring

Particles traveling clockwise

Accelerator is underground to shield it from cosmic rays

Particles collide at this point

Nature's glue

In addition to looking for the building blocks of matter, scientists are searching for the forces that glue matter together. They currently believe that quarks are bound together by particles called gluons. They think each gluon exists for only a moment, making it very difficult to detect. Fleeting particles, including gluons, could be responsible for every force in the universe—even gravity.

Annihilation

Every type of particle in the universe has a mirror particle that has completely opposite characteristics. Anything made from these mirror particles is called antimatter. When matter and antimatter meet, they destroy each other in a burst of pure energy. Scientists call this event annihilation. In the large electron positron (LEP) collider at CERN, scientists watch electrons and their antiparticles, positrons, at the moment they annihilate each other.

△ As particles get faster and faster, it becomes harder to steer them around a curve. The ring-shaped LEP collider at CERN is huge so that its curve is very gentle.

▷ At the core of this new accelerator, protons travel in opposite directions around two pipes that lie side by side. Once they are going fast enough, the two pipes are linked together so the protons can collide.

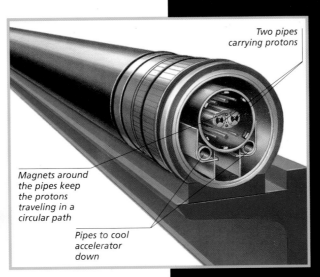

Two pipes carrying protons

Magnets around the pipes keep the protons traveling in a circular path

Pipes to cool accelerator down

Power

Fusion • Wind power • Solar cars
Lightsails • Biomass • Wave energy

People use the world's energy sources to heat their buildings, to fuel their cars, and to make TVs, stoves, and countless other machines work. But many of these fuels, such as coal, oil, and gas, are in limited supply. That is why physicists and engineers are looking for new energy sources. In particular, they are looking for ones that are clean, safe, and available in unlimited quantities.

High-temperature fusion

Physicists around the world are trying to build a power station that works just like the Sun. The Sun is largely made up of hydrogen atoms. It generates energy when these atoms fuse together at temperatures over 10 million degrees centigrade to make atoms of helium. When the hydrogen atoms fuse, they release huge bursts of energy, as well as stray particles called neutrons. All the raw ingredients of this fusion reaction are nontoxic and easy to make. The waste neutrons can be made harmless, too.

◁ The rotors of these wind turbines move with the wind. The best wind turbines can convert about a third of the wind energy that reaches them into electricity.

Using the wind

For centuries, people have harnessed the wind to power mills, boats, and other machines. Over the last few decades, they have used the wind to generate electricity, too. The machines that turn wind energy into electricity are called wind turbines. In a strong wind, a turbine can create enough energy to power several homes.

△ The Honda *Dream* solar car

Solar power

Covered in solar cells (tiles that convert sunlight into electricity), the car above runs without a single drop of gasoline. The car is called the Honda *Dream* and is powered entirely by the Sun. Its streamlined, teardrop-shaped body can cruise at 35 miles per hour, even with two passengers. Cars such as the *Dream* are only prototypes, built for solar-powered races. But the engineers developing them are learning how to make vehicles that run on little or no fuel.

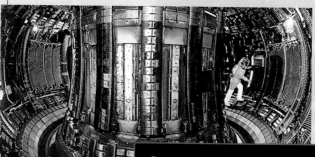

△ ▷ **A reactor (above) in which controlled nuclear fusion (right) took place would be a very clean and safe source of power.**

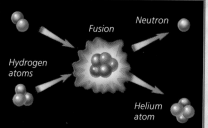

Fusion

Neutron

Hydrogen atoms

Helium atom

Photon power

Spaceships may one day travel vast distances across the solar system, powered by light from the Sun. All light is made from streams of photons. These strange particles have no mass but lots of energy. Some scientists have proposed putting a giant but very lightweight sail in the path of photons from the Sun. In theory, the photons would collide with this lightsail and push it along. A lightsail would start moving very slowly, but would steadily accelerate (speed up). Recent calculations have suggested it could travel from Earth to Mars in around 400 days.

▽ **Some people have considered powering spacecraft using the solar wind (see page 38). The solar wind is the stream of electrons and protons that comes from the Sun. However, it would not produce as much power as the Sun's photons. It is also highly irregular, arriving in huge bursts during solar flares.**

▽ **A lightsail could be made from a film of aluminum, backed by thin plastic.**

Biomass

Across the world, people don't all have the same energy demands. The city of New York, for example, uses as much gas in a week as the whole of Africa uses in a year. People in developing countries live with very low fuel demands. Many of them rely entirely on biomass (burning wood, crops, and dung) for energy.

▽ **Wood is still the main fuel for billions of people around the world.**

Clean energy?

The oceans, which cover seven-tenths of the planet, are huge, untapped energy sources. They are powered by heat from the Sun. This produces waves, tides, and currents that could be used to drive turbines. Wave energy may seem like a clean source of power, but it does have some potential drawbacks. For example, tides that have been tapped for their energy move more slowly through estuaries and other coastal areas. Many animals rely on moving tides and estuaries for food and transportation. The unnaturally sluggish tide would make it harder for them to survive.

Nanotechnology

Nanomachines • Nanobuilding • Micromachines
Keeping in touch • Microrobots

Imagine a machine, smaller than a speck of dust, that has thousands of moving parts. Amazingly, some chemists and engineers are already making machines just like this. They have found ways to build moving parts that are only a few atoms in size. These tiny devices have huge potential. Some could become microscopic factories; others could be used as robots that swim through the human bloodstream doing repair work.

△▽ **Every bristle on a flea's back (above) is ten times as long as this nanoguitar (below). The guitar's movable strings are only 100 atoms wide.**

How small is nano?

It's mind-boggling to think about the smallest machines ever made. Each one is a few billionths of a yard in size—a million of them, end to end, would fit into the full stop at the end of this sentence. We can't see these nanomachines directly with our eyes. We have to map out their shape using an electron microscope, a machine that detects the bumps made by individual atoms. Engineers are finding ways to pack millions of nanomachines onto a silicon wafer no bigger than a postage stamp. They are also making computer chips with microscopic moving parts.

Nanoconstruction

Some of the most ambitious researchers are putting nanomachines together, one atom at a time. These chemists design their machines using powerful computer programs. A few try to turn their designs into real nanomachines by trial and error, mixing the raw ingredients together until they end up with the cluster of atoms they expect. Others make nanomachines using a scanning tunneling microscope (STM). An STM is a machine that lets them "see" individual atoms. A beam of particles, called electrons, fired from the tip of an STM, can be used to move individual atoms around, just like bricks in a microscopic construction kit.

△ **Designed on a computer, these nanocogs are a few millionths of a millimeter in diameter. They are made from individual atoms.**

Inside the body

Soon, minuscule machines could be put to work inside the body. Some could even mimic living parts of the body itself. A microrobot, for example, could swim through arteries and clear away any blockages. A nanocomputer could pick up and send messages, just like a neuron (nerve cell). Millions of these messages could be used together to repair a damaged brain. They could help people to regain fully active lives after suffering strokes or head injuries. Today, many people with diabetes have to take regular doses of insulin to keep their bodies working properly. In the future, a microscopic factory could make insulin automatically. Put inside a diabetic's body, the microfactory would constantly monitor body conditions and supply the correct dose of insulin at the right time.

◁ **This miniature submarine, traveling through a human artery, has a moving propeller. It was built to show how micromachines could be used inside the body.**

▷ **As it beams images into the eye, the microprojector on these glasses gives the wearer a continual picture of a virtual world.**

Tiny machines

So far, researchers have had most success etching tiny machines from wafers of silicon. This process made the cogs you can see below. Engineers transfer a pattern of the shape they are making onto a silicon wafer. If they blast the wafer with a beam of ions (atoms with electrical charge), they can make usable micromachines—machines that are a few thousandths of a millimeter in size.

▽ **Each of these microcogs is smaller than a grain of pollen.**

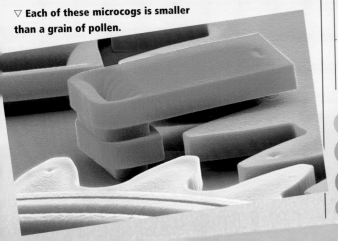

Keeping in touch

Using micromachines, computer interfaces (see page 9) can be made smaller and lighter than ever before. For example, it's already possible to buy a tiny video projector that works using microscopic, spinning mirrors. Small enough to mount on a pair of glasses, this projector can beam images directly into a user's eye. Micromachines can also make virtual worlds (worlds created on computers) seem far more realistic. If they mimic parts of the body that give us our senses, they allow us to experience these worlds in many different ways. A micromachine that plugs into our nasal cells, for example, could give us a convincing sense of smell. Micromachines woven into gloves and suits could produce a virtual sense of touch.

New materials

Smart materials • Shape memory alloys
Artificial diamonds • Electronic paper • Superfluids

New materials, developed in the laboratory, are now being put to use. Nanotechnology, for example, enables us to make "smart materials" that remember their shape, respond to their surroundings, or even self-destruct at the end of their life span. As people discover more about making new materials, the way we engineer buildings, factories, and tools could change forever.

△ The light-sensitive glass covering a skyscraper keeps the light levels inside the building constant.

Smart buildings

Buildings put together with smart materials can respond to their surroundings, almost like living things. A museum covered with light-sensitive glass, for example, can darken on bright days to stop the treasures inside from fading. A temporary building made with smart bricks could turn itself to rubble when it is time to pull it down. Construction engineers and architects are only just beginning to explore the possibilities that smart materials offer.

Materials with memory

Dented objects made from the metal Nitinol can simply be warmed back into shape. That's because Nitinol is a shape memory alloy (SMA)—a metal that can remember its original size and shape. Nitinol is a mixture of nickel, titanium, and other metals. Its atoms are arranged in a compact, rigid structure. If a Nitinol object is dented or twisted, gentle heat will make its atoms spring back into their original arrangement. Nitinol has already been used to make glasses frames, aircraft parts, dental braces, and tweezers. SMAs have also been used to repair the famous church of St. Francis in Assisi, Italy, after it was damaged in the earthquakes of 1997.

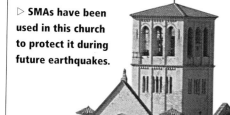

▷ SMAs have been used in this church to protect it during future earthquakes.

Diamond crystals

Priceless diamonds, mined from the earth, can be replaced by ones made in the laboratory. When scientists make artificial diamonds, they don't just produce another material that looks like the real thing. They make genuine diamond crystals by subjecting graphite to the temperatures and pressures found in the Earth's core. Diamond, the hardest known material, is almost perfectly transparent. Artificial diamonds are replacing real ones in industrial metal-cutters, coatings for machine parts, and even sensors for new types of X-ray machine.

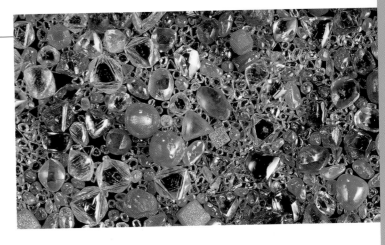

▷ **This photograph shows real diamonds mixed up with artificial diamonds made in the laboratory. They are so alike it is almost impossible to tell them apart.**

▽ **Gentle warming in the palm of the hand makes these Nitinol glasses frames spring back into shape.**

Reusable paper

Engineers are developing a sheet of paper that can be wiped clean over and over again. Called electronic paper, you can write on it, read it, then roll it up, and stick it in your pocket. But you can also plug it straight into a computer to download pictures and words. In close-up, electronic paper is made of millions of tiny, rolling beads. Each one is black on one side and white on the other. Electric signals roll each of the beads around independently to make up a picture from millions of black-and-white dots. When you write on the electronic paper with an electronic wand, it makes an electric signal that rolls the paper's beads to record your words.

Tiny, rolling beads

Beads black side up to form A

Bizarre fluids

Some of the most bizarre materials under investigation are called superfluids. These fluids move without any friction and can even roll uphill. So far, scientists have only found superfluids that exist at very low temperatures. A type of helium, for example, becomes a superfluid at around −455° F, almost the coldest temperature that can exist. There seems to be no end to the strangeness of superfluids—even sound flows through them faster in one direction than in another.

△ **Electronic paper is made up of millions of tiny beads, half black, half white.**

SEE ALSO

Restless planet

Long-term forecasts • Solar flares
Global warming • Earthquakes

When a region is hit by a natural disaster, we're reminded how difficult it is to predict the weather. Air, oceans, land, and the Sun create the weather on Earth. Scientists are discovering how these elements work together to produce the world's ever-changing weather.

◁▽ **Satellite pictures of weather patterns help weather forecasters.**

Problems from space

The Sun is the ultimate source of all energy on Earth. But it's a supply that continually varies. The Sun is an extremely hot ball of gas that pulsates all the time, throwing off huge flares of particles. Within a few hours or days, material from these solar flares reaches Earth, where it can damage electrical parts in satellites, computers, and other electronic equipment. NASA has put a satellite, called SOHO, between the Earth and the Sun to warn us of any large solar flares on the way. It will enable people to protect vulnerable equipment before particles from solar flares arrive.

Predicting the weather

It's difficult to predict what the weather will be like a few days in the future. Long-range forecasts are even harder to get right. But farmers, fishermen, oil-platform builders, and many other people would find it helpful to know the weather next week, month, or year. If oil companies knew when it was going to be calm, for example, they could work out the safest time to build new rigs. Many meteorologists (weather scientists) use satellites to monitor weather patterns on the planet. This work is called remote sensing. The CloudSat project uses three satellites to check on clouds. Scientists hope information from CloudSat will help them to understand how clouds influence the world's climate.

▷ **Many crop-destroying pests thrive in hot weather. If farmers knew in advance from long-range forecasts when to expect cooler spells, they could decide when to spray less pesticide.**

◁ Particles rip from the Sun during a violent solar flare (below left). The SOHO satellite (top left) can warn us that some of these particles will soon be reaching Earth.

Violent weather

People around the world are concerned that the climate is getting warmer. Global warming (see pages 32–33) would increase the severity of Earth's weather, as well as the planet's temperature. A warmer world would probably have greater temperature differences between the poles and the equator. For this reason, it would have much stronger winds and ocean currents. Storms, floods, and heavy rainfall would be far more common. However, scientists find it hard to tell the difference between ordinary variations in the weather and changes in the world's climate. As the energy from the Sun is also continually varying, it's even harder to tell when the Earth's climate has permanently altered. Is the world getting warmer simply because the Sun is becoming more active? When the Sun goes into a cooler spell, will global warming be reversed?

◁ A girl and a boy collect water after a flash flood in Bangladesh. When the Earth acts violently, it can devastate lives and homes.

Water and earthquakes

Water in the air and oceans helps to create the weather. But water below ground could be responsible for some of the world's earthquakes, too. For example, in the hills of Lesotho, South Africa, water seeping from an artificial dam forced cracks between rocks to grow wider, causing a minor tremor. Water may also have helped to trigger the great earthquake that devastated the city of Kobe, Japan, in 1995. Studies of the rocks around Kobe, 11 miles below ground, showed that water had built up inside them. The water pressed on the rocks around it, breaking them apart. As the earthquake struck, the city was flooded with muddy, salt water. This water had probably seeped under the gravel that had been put into the sea to make Kobe's port. When the earth shook, gaps appeared between the stones. The seawater was able to seep straight through these gaps, flooding the city.

△ Sections of this freeway in California collapsed during a 1989 earthquake when the wet, muddy ground below it wobbled like jelly.

SEE ALSO

How and when will our world die?	50–51
Vulcanologist	53–55
Glossary	78–81

Chaos and chance

Chaos theory • Chaotic systems • Advertising
Computer graphics • Fractals

Mathematicians have been finding more reliable ways to forecast the behavior of seemingly unpredictable things, such as the weather, the stock exchange, and election voters. They call their new methods of forecasting "chaos theory." It is already helping them to predict the unpredictable.

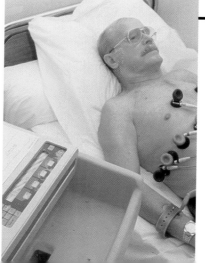

Complexity

Chaos theory enables us to find patterns in things that seem to be completely chaotic. The wind is an example. Rather than assuming it's completely unpredictable, chaos theory considers the wind to be made up of billions of tiny, separate air molecules. Each molecule moves in an entirely predictable way, but it would be impractical to predict the behavior of every single one. However, it is possible to search for the general patterns of behavior of this extremely complex system. Mathematicians use chaos theory to do this. It lets them forecast the overall, future behavior of all the air molecules in an area—in other words, the future direction and strength of the wind. An election is another example of a chaotic system. The final result depends on the votes cast by thousands of individuals. Each person's vote seems to have a small effect on the outcome. But a single vote that decides a very closely fought election can have a huge effect.

△ **Identical sums in chaos theory can be applied to completely different-looking systems. The same calculations can be used to predict the timing of water droplets from a leaky faucet (above) and the timing of irregular beats of a diseased heart (right).**

Prediction

Dripping faucets and other things that can be understood using chaos theory are called chaotic systems. Although they are called chaotic, they aren't really like that. They are simply made up of billions of smaller working parts that make the problem of predicting their behavior very complex. Chaos theory is a powerful way to search out patterns in these seemingly disordered systems. People are already attempting to use chaos theory to predict future hurricanes and the spread of infectious diseases.

Creating crazes

▽ **An election is an interesting example of a chaotic system.**

In addition to forecasting real events, chaos theory can be used to calculate the best way to influence them. An advertising company, for example, tried to use chaos theory to turn a toy into a craze. They hoped news of the new toy would spread between school children, just like the flu! Using chaos theory, they estimated the best times and places to introduce their products to a few children in order to start the craze.

▷ **Crazes for toys such as Pokémon can spread across the planet as fast as any virus.**

Flocking birds

△ **Using ideas from chaos theory, a computer programmer can make a flock of cartoon birds move just like the real thing.**

Chaos theory can be used to make computer graphics that move like living things. People use it, for example, to animate creatures moving together—a herd of charging wildebeest, a team of football players, or a flock of birds. They know how one bird flies, for instance, when there are other birds around it. It would take a lot of computing power to calculate the movements of every bird in a flock. It would take even more to put the movements of dozens of birds together, frame by frame. It's much easier to use chaos theory to work out the changing, overall pattern of the flock.

Computer-generated scenes

The hedges, trees, grass, clouds, and other background pictures in computer games are often produced using mathematics. The computer draws them using simple patterns that repeat in constantly changing ways. Patterns like these are called fractals. One fractal can produce many different, finely detailed, natural-looking shapes. The shapes may look like randomly generated pictures, but they are all made mathematically. Fractals are an example of chaos theory in action. A tiny shift in their starting point can change their final look noticeably. To store a fractal picture, you just need to know the basic fractal shape and the way you will be shifting it. This takes up very little memory in a computer.

SEE ALSO

The information age	9
Are any machines smarter than humans?	42–43
Glossary	78–81

◁ **The background landscapes of this computer game look different every time you play. That's because the computer varies the starting point of the fractals that create these elements.**

Earth's future

Climate change • Human activity
Greenhouse gases • Epidemics
Global cooling • The ozone layer

The biggest questions facing weather scientists concern the Earth's climate. On average, the Earth is around 1.8° F warmer today than it was in 1860. Scientists are still arguing over why this global warming is happening and how long it will continue.

Heating up

The weather in any part of the world will always vary from year to year. But climate change is about more than short-term variations. Temperature measurements around the globe have shown that the world has been getting warmer over the last 150 years. Some scientists think global warming is just part of the Earth's natural variation. Others think it is due to polluting chemicals that people have put into the air. We pump large amounts of chemicals into the air when we burn fuel, for example in power stations and cars.

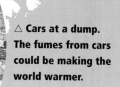

△ Cars at a dump. The fumes from cars could be making the world warmer.

◁ A cloud of smog hangs over Mexico City, in Central America. Smog is caused by burning fuels such as petrol.

The human influence

Scientists still don't know all the reasons for global warming and they can't agree if human activity is the biggest cause. When coal, gasoline, or gas are burned to generate power, carbon dioxide gas is produced. We pump most carbon dioxide into the air when we run airplanes, cars, light bulbs, air conditioners, refrigerators, and any other machines that need lots of power. Scientists know that carbon dioxide and other chemicals in the air trap heat from the Sun, making the Earth warmer. However, they still aren't sure how easily the Earth can overcome the warming effects of these chemicals. So many factors influence the Earth's climate, it's almost impossible to unravel their individual effects. It's also hard to work out what will heat or cool the planet. If the world gets slightly warmer, for example, more of the oceans will evaporate, adding moisture to the air. This moisture may create more clouds which may shield the Earth from the Sun, lessening any warming effect.

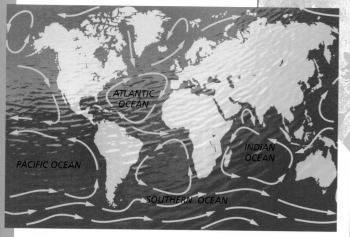

ATLANTIC OCEAN

INDIAN OCEAN

PACIFIC OCEAN

SOUTHERN OCEAN

△ Ocean currents move heat around the globe. Warmer oceans would create different currents, spreading heat differently.

▷ **This environment-friendly radio is powered by winding it up and boosted by energy from the Sun.**

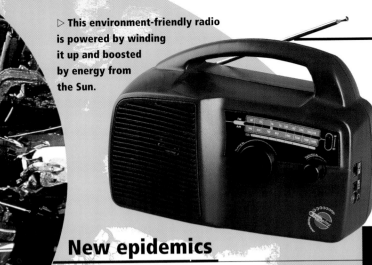

Earth-friendly power

While debates about global warming continue, many people are trying to cut down on greenhouse gases that trap heat in the air. Cars, air conditioners, refrigerators, TVs, and many other powered goods are greenhouse gas producers. Even if they don't actually make the gases, they use electricity from power stations that produce them. Many people are looking at cleaner forms of power, including ones that are greenhouse gas free.

New epidemics

If the world's climate is changing, diseases could be spreading across different parts of the world too. In a warmer world, more areas would experience tropical temperatures. These areas would be more likely to suffer diseases that thrive in heat. In September 1991, in New York City, there was an outbreak of encephalitis. This deadly disease is usually found much farther south where the climate is warmer. Pest controllers had to spray many areas of the city with pesticide to kill mosquitoes that were carrying ticks infected by this disease.

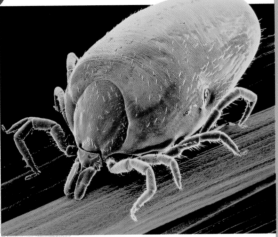

▷ **Bad luck caused this tick to arrive in New York. But global warming could cause more tropical diseases to spread to northerly areas.**

Natural events

Our actions may be making the world warmer—but some natural events can cool it down. One example is the eruption of Mount Pinatubo, a volcano in the Philippines. When Pinatubo erupted in 1991, it threw huge amounts of extremely fine ash into the atmosphere blocking out many of the Sun's rays and cooling the climate by around 1.8° F. The effects lasted for many months. Some scientists argue that natural events like this counteract the effects of any human activity.

Ozone thinning

Chemicals we have put into the air have already caused damage to the Earth's protective ozone layer. At 9 to 31 miles above the ground, this layer of gas shields the Earth from some of the Sun's ultraviolet rays. Too much ultraviolet light can burn the skin, triggering cancers. It can also harm the eyes. Governments around the world have agreed to stop using chlorofluorocarbons (CFCs), chemicals that cause most damage to the ozone layer. CFCs were used in many refrigerators and aerosol cans. If we stopped putting ozone-destroying chemicals into the air, the ozone layer would eventually mend.

△ **The blue areas on this image show the ozone layer thinning over the South Pole.**

◁ **Scientists take samples deep in the Antarctic ice to assess the world's climate over thousands of years. The thinning of the ozone layer was originally discovered by scientists monitoring the Antarctic atmosphere.**

Biodiversity

Cultural diversity • Rare plants • Sustainability
Keystone species • Seed banks

Around 30 million different plant and animal species live on Earth. Humans make up just one tiny part of the planet's interconnected web of living things, called the biosphere. Our activity can have a huge impact on other species. Some of our actions have led to a number of plants and animals becoming extinct. People are now looking for ways to preserve the Earth's biodiversity—the variety of living things on the planet.

△ An Inuit family drive their dog sled over sea ice. The land of the Inuit used to be part of Canada, but has now become an independent state. The Inuits hope this will help them preserve their ways of life.

Human biodiversity

Many human traditions are in danger of extinction, just like rare plants or animals. There are various reasons why some human cultures are in decline. People from poorer countries adopt the languages of more powerful ones, for example, in order to find work. Some scientists consider the variety of people, languages, and traditions to be a type of biodiversity. Any culture can contribute to human knowledge and understanding, so every one deserves protection.

Plant treasures

We have every reason to protect rare plants across the globe. Countless animal species would become extinct if the plants they relied on disappeared. Many people around the world use local plants for food, fuel, medicines, or shelter. Recently, scientists have become concerned that some endangered plants could turn out to be sources of chemicals for curing widespread diseases. Around a quarter of modern medicinal drugs were originally developed from plants. A few scientists are combing the world for plants that could be used to fight cancer, AIDS, and other big killers. They have already had some success with a slow-growing tree called the Pacific yew. In its bark, they discovered a drug that can fight certain types of cancers. This has now been developed into a powerful cancer drug called Taxol.

Taxol is used to treat some types of cancers

Pacific yew tree

Human impact

People use just under half the world's land to grow crops. We fish the oceans, chop down trees for fuel and shelter, and make our cities bigger every year. Intensive activities such as these have a huge impact on the planet. They destroy or change the natural habitat of many plants and animals, making it difficult for them to survive. Some activities can lead directly to the extinction of certain species because they consume plants or animals faster than offspring can replace them. Many people are trying to live more sustainably, using the Earth's resources without endangering their future supply.

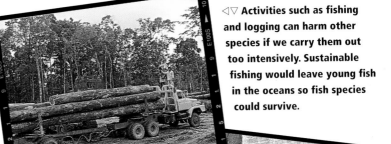

◁▽ Activities such as fishing and logging can harm other species if we carry them out too intensively. Sustainable fishing would leave young fish in the oceans so fish species could survive.

◁ When keystone species like this sea otter are in danger, many other local species are at risk.

Vital species

Some animals have such an important role in their local habitat that even small changes in their numbers can be catastrophic. Animals like these are called keystone species. A well-known example is the sea otter. Living along the northern coasts of the Pacific Ocean, this creature feeds on the sea urchin which, in turn, eats a type of seaweed called kelp. Each sea otter eats many sea urchins, and each sea urchin survives on large amounts of kelp. If the number of sea otters goes down slightly, many more sea urchins survive, so the amount of kelp reduces dramatically.

◁ The plant-based cancer drug Taxol highlights the importance of preserving biodiversity.

Saving seeds

Within 50 years, a quarter of all the world's plant species could be extinct. Scientists realize they will have to work swiftly to preserve plant biodiversity—many forests, meadows, wetlands, and other plant habitats are already disappearing fast. That's why some countries have set up seed banks. These banks are stores for the seeds of many thousands of different plant species. Seeds can be preserved for hundreds of years, and very little space is needed to keep plant species alive as simple seeds. When they add a plant species to the seed bank, researchers try to collect seeds from many different plants, growing at more than one location. They research seeds while they are in storage to learn more about the Earth's plant life. They examine the genetic codes of plants, for example, to learn more about their evolution. If a plant in the wild is in danger of extinction, it can be rescued using seeds from a seed bank.

◁ Seeds stored in a seed bank are kept very cool to preserve them for many decades.

SEE ALSO

Are we still evolving?	60–61
Plants that cure	84–85
Glossary	90–93

Space-time

Space-time effects • Twin Paradox
Looking back • The multiverse • Black holes

Look into the night sky and you can see some of the stars in our universe. You see each one because light has traveled a vast distance from the star to your eyes. Every day, you travel much shorter distances—for example, when you take a walk. But you, the stars, light, and everything else in the universe are also on another journey. All are continuously traveling through time. As we travel through both space and time, scientists think of them as two parts of one thing. They call it space-time.

Travel through space-time

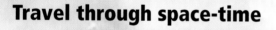

Around 100 years ago, the scientist Albert Einstein made a fascinating discovery about travel through space-time. One aspect of his discovery concerned time itself. His discovery seems very peculiar at first because it goes against our usual experience. One way to explain it is to imagine a boy on Earth, talking to his brother, an astronaut, on a cellular phone. The astronaut brother is in a fast-moving spaceship that is whizzing past Earth. Amazingly, the boy on Earth notices that his brother is talking and moving very slowly. The faster the spaceship goes, the bigger this problem becomes. This isn't because the cellular phone is faulty. To the brother on Earth, time itself is progressing more slowly on the spaceship. Time changes like this happen whenever an object moves relative to an observer, no matter how fast it is going. But these changes are only big enough to be noticeable if the object travels very fast—almost as fast as light. So far, we have not built a spaceship that can travel at such a speed.

...eats breakfast.
Now I've missed the bus!
Shall I walk to school?

YES

...half an hour later.
Aagh, I've overslept! Have I got time for breakfast?

...half an hour later. Well, I caught the bus... but now it's broken down...

NO

Morning!
Shall I get up?

NO

YES

...gets up.
Nice and early.
Shall I walk to school?

YES

...half an hour later.
It was a lovely day when I set out – now it's pouring. Shall I shelter in the shop?

THE TWIN PARADOX

Space-time puzzle

One interesting space-time puzzle is called the Twin Paradox. It concerns twin boys, one of whom is sent away from Earth in a fast spaceship for 80 years. If the boy left on Earth could check his brother's watch, he would find it was moving more slowly than his own. During his brother's mission, he feels 80 years go by while his brother feels only 40. What would the twins look like when they met up at the end of the mission?

Looking back in time

The distances between the stars are staggering. Light, the fastest thing in the universe, takes over four years to reach us from Proxima Centauri, the nearest star to the Sun. It takes 15 billion years to travel from the most distant stars in the universe. Hubble, a telescope orbiting the Earth, can see stars this far away. As it picks up light that left these stars 15 billion years ago, it shows us how the stars looked at that point in the past—how they looked at the beginning of time.

◁ **This image of distant galaxies was taken by the Hubble space telescope. The redder objects are the oldest stars.**

...goes to store.
This was a bad idea!
The store has been raided
by armed robbers...

NO

...waits for bus.
Now I'm really late! I
wish I could teleport
myself to school...

YES

NO
...on the way to school.
I'm hungry! Is there time to go
to the store to buy
something to eat?

NO

...in shop.
Well I'm nice and dry
now... but I'm also
late for school...

YES

NO

...at school.
Phew, just made it,
but I'm soaked to the
skin.

...11 o'clock.
Now I'm really hungry!

△ **Perhaps you step into
a new universe every time you
make a decision in your life.**

△ **This disk of stardust at the center of galaxy NGC 7052 could be circling a black hole. Scientists have calculated that this black hole would need to be as heavy as 300 million suns.**

The Great Annihilator

Black holes are some of the most fascinating features in the universe. Each one is created by an extremely dense cluster of matter—for example, a dead star that has collapsed into a ball just a few miles across. A black hole is so dense that it creates enormous gravitational forces which pull everything toward it. A black hole, called the Great Annihilator, at the center of our own galaxy seems to be pulling stars toward it. Not even a beam of light can travel fast enough to escape a black hole if it gets too close. A few people have speculated that black holes, joined together, could form short cuts through space-time itself—or even routes to other universes in a multiverse.

Many universes

Most scientists agree that our universe began in a sudden, colossal explosion called the Big Bang. Space, time, energy, and everything else were all created in this event that happened around 15 billion years ago. Over time, the universe gradually expanded from a single point, the center of the explosion, to become what it is today. Scientists still don't know where the material of the Big Bang emerged from. Perhaps our universe is just one part of a giant "multiverse"—a cluster of universes, each created from something larger by its own Big Bang. A few mathematicians have wondered whether we create a new universe every time we make a decision. Their theories suggest that we step from universe to universe all the time.

SEE ALSO

How did space and time begin?	39
What are the biggest unanswered questions?	52
Glossary	78–81

Speeding into the future

Future designs • Solar wind • Quantum telepathy

As scientists develop their understanding of the universe, they are imagining new ways to travel through space. Will any of their ideas lead to working spacecraft that can carry people to and from distant stars in the future?

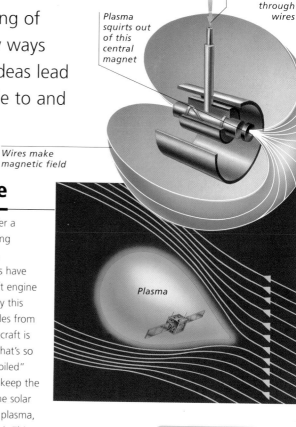

Helium gas heated to form a plasma

Electric current runs through wires

Plasma squirts out of this central magnet

Wires make magnetic field

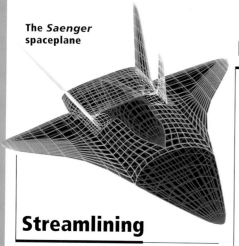

The *Saenger* spaceplane

Streamlining

Spaceplanes of the future are designed to travel high in Earth's atmosphere, then go into orbit, making swift journeys around the globe. As they spend part of their journey in the air, spaceplanes have to be streamlined just like ordinary aircraft. This spaceplane, called the *Saenger*, has swept-back wings that help it to travel safely at four times the speed of sound.

Plasma drive

The solar wind could offer a practical way to travel long distances through space. Recently, a few engineers have tried to build a spacecraft engine that could be powered by this irregular stream of particles from the Sun. Inside the spacecraft is a ball of plasma—a gas that's so hot its electrons have "boiled" away. Powerful magnets keep the plasma in place. When the solar wind comes close to this plasma, it repels it (pushes it away). This pushes the spacecraft along.

▽ **Unlike the crew in the TV show "Star Trek," we can't find a way to teleport or travel faster than light.**

Plasma

△ **The solar wind and the ball of plasma in the spacecraft repel each other, pushing the spacecraft along.**

SEE ALSO

How did space and time begin?	39
Are we alone in the universe?	46–47
Space exploration	76–77

Science fiction travel

Science fiction writers have written about traveling to a destination instantly, using a "teleporter." Scientists have imagined teleportation, too. They already know that single particles, bound together in a special way, can keep in touch over any distance. If one of these "entangled" particles is spun around in one direction, the other spins the opposite way. The two particles spin at the exactly same time, even if they are many galaxies apart. Sadly, scientists don't think this effect could be used to teleport across the universe. This form of instant communication, called quantum telepathy, disappears as soon as you try to measure the movements of either particle!

FAQs

FAQs

How did **space and time** begin?

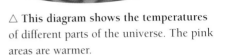

△ This diagram shows the temperatures of different parts of the universe. The pink areas are warmer.

The universe began about 15 billion years ago when it expanded from a tiny central point called a singularity. At that moment, known as the Big Bang, space, time, and the raw materials of everything were created. Imagine a universe packed into a singularity so minuscule that it would fit into a grain of sand a thousand billion billion times over!

▽ Taken by the Hubble space telescope, this image is of a giant cloud of dust called the Eagle nebula.

How quickly did the stars and planets form?

The universe has never stopped expanding, and as it grows, it cools. In its early life, it was too hot for stars and planets to form. After about a million years of cooling, stars were able to develop from clouds of particles. Gravity pulled these particles together into clumps. As the clumps became larger, they pulled on more and more particles until they formed giant stars. The planets probably formed from the debris around the stars.

▽ This nebula (cloud of particles) is so far away, we see it as it looked around 13 billion years ago. Stars can form from a nebula like this.

Why do so many scientists believe the Big Bang theory?

The universe is teeming with evidence of a Big Bang. The empty space between the stars, for example, is exactly the temperature scientists would expect it to be after an explosion about 15 billion years ago. Another piece of evidence is that wherever you are in the universe, all the stars are moving away from you. This is not happening fast enough to see—but it can be picked up using radio telescopes. They're moving away because everything is expanding from the center of the Big Bang.

▽ Every speck in this photograph is a distant galaxy. Images like this, taken by Hubble, help us to discover more about the history of the universe.

Can
we make **designer babies?**

Scientists have just completed the Human Genome Project, a worldwide project to trace all the genes that make us human. As scientists learn how genes vary from person to person, they are discovering how some of them affect our health. Meanwhile, they are also developing new skills in genetic engineering. In theory, they can use these skills to change the genes of people, including unborn babies, and alter their future health.

How can genetics help us to engineer humans?

There are two ways we can alter human genes: somatic and germline. In somatic therapies, some of the cells of a living person are altered. These therapies have already been developed for a few genetic diseases. For example, people with cystic fibrosis, a genetic illness that clogs up the lungs, can take a somatic therapy in an inhaler. This alters the cells lining the lungs so they produce less clogging mucus. Germline therapy involves changing the genes of an embryo—a cluster of cells that can develop inside its mother into an unborn child. This therapy permanently alters the genes in every one of a person's cells.

▽ Unlike somatic therapy, germline therapy changes every one of a person's cells—including the sperm or eggs. This means that changes made by germline therapy are passed down to the next generation.

△ Genetic scientists are able to screen human sperm before they meet an egg. For example, they can tell which ones are most likely to produce females (dyed pink in this picture to make them show up).

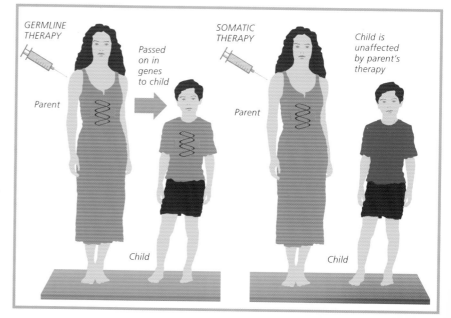

GERMLINE THERAPY

Parent

Passed on in genes to child

Child

SOMATIC THERAPY

Parent

Child is unaffected by parent's therapy

Child

Will it be possible to engineer any trait, including intelligence and personality?

Fortunately, you are formed by far more than your genes. Traits such as intelligence, personality, interests, and sense of humor have as much to do with the way you are brought up, the things you have seen and read, and the friends you hang around with. Even the simplest physical traits, like the quality of your teeth, are due to interactions between several genes—as well as your diet. It's unlikely that anyone will be able to engineer traits such as sparkling teeth, let alone intelligence or personality.

▷ **This cluster of fertilized** cells, called an embryo, has the potential to grow into a fully developed baby. It is already possible to check the genes of an embryo such as this.

What laws are in place to control this science?

Research into human genetics is progressing so rapidly that governments have to work fast to keep the laws on this science up to date. While some countries ban human germline therapy altogether, others have committees to judge each new advance on its own merits. Recently, 186 countries signed a United Nations declaration on human genetics, agreeing to avoid any genetic engineering that threatens the rights of individuals.

What are the benefits and the risks?

A few people carry genes that are strongly linked to cystic fibrosis, breast cancer, or other fatal diseases. For them, germline therapy offers enormous benefits. It can eliminate the genes that cause them and their children so much harm. But germline therapy also carries many risks. Unlike any other type of medicine, its effects can last for generations. A person's altered genes will be passed on to their children and grandchildren. This makes it difficult to deal with problems if new genes are faulty in any way. And will the human race gradually evolve into two groups: people who can afford germline therapy and people who cannot?

◁ **People disagree about what makes a good** quality of life. There's a danger that human genetic engineering may make us less tolerant of human variety, for example physical disability.

SEE ALSO

Breaking the code	12–13
Genetics breakthroughs	74–75
Glossary	78–81

Are any machines smarter than **humans?**

△ The human brain can tell that this is the same girl, despite the different hairstyles, but computers are easily fooled by such differences.

On May 11, 1997, Gary Kasparov, the World Chess Champion, was beaten by an unlikely opponent. The match, which made world headlines, pitted Kasparov's wits against a computer. The computer was loaded with chess-playing software, a program called Deep Blue. When the news broke, reporters around the world asked if machines had become smarter than humans. Meanwhile, scientists were still wondering if any machine could ever think.

▷ A human chess player occasionally has moments of inspiration, but a chess computer can only work out the consequences of every possible move.

❓ What are the smartest machines in use today?

The answer to this question depends on how you measure smartness. Supercomputers have the most thinking power (see page 9). However, software programs called neural networks that learn and adapt are probably the smartest around. People are experimenting with them to control robots, find and track moving objects, and understand human speech (see pages 10–11).

Kasparov

Deep Blue

❓ How smart is a computer?

If you measure how fast a computer works and how much information it can store in its memory, you can get a rough idea of its thinking power. On this basis, a typical desktop computer has the same thinking power as a bee (see pages 70–71)! But a computer is only as smart as the software that runs on it. Software is the computer program that makes it play chess, puts pictures on the page, or allows you to write a letter. Unlike the human brain, software is dedicated to performing a limited range of tasks, according to a set of rules. In this respect, no computer has ever been as smart as a human.

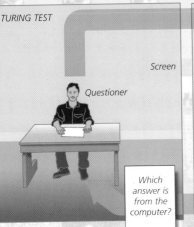

TURING TEST

Same question sent to person and computer

Screen

Questioner

Computer replies

Person replies

Which answer is from the computer?

How can you tell if a machine is intelligent?

The test for machine intelligence was devised by Alan Turing (see page 11). Turing worked out a test that involved an interviewer asking a computer and a person questions on any topic. If the interviewer couldn't tell which answers came from the human and which from the computer, then the computer was truly intelligent. It was a thinking machine. No computer built so far has come close to passing the Turing test.

Does it understand?

To explain why this is a more difficult question than "Can a machine think?," the mathematician Graham Searle thought up an experiment called the Chinese Room. It used an English speaker, sitting in a box, equipped with a Chinese–English and English–Chinese translating machine. The person in the box could take in Chinese questions and use the translator to answer them in Chinese, without knowing any Chinese at all. People outside the box wouldn't know that he didn't understand Chinese. A machine could seem to think, without truly understanding, in just the same way.

△ **Alan Turing asked** the question "Can a computer think?" as early as 1950. This is his test.

▷ **Children color in** a map in a geography lesson at school. Unlike a computer, a human brain can actually change its internal connections as it learns.

CHINESE ROOM

Chinese question in

Translator Chinese-English

Translator English-Chinese

Chinese answer out

English answer

Is it possible to have a conversation with a machine?

A few computer programs can obey spoken commands and recognize spoken words. None of them can do the much harder job of figuring out what the words mean— whether they are spoken or in type. The human ability to understand speech is astounding. As we listen to someone else, we experience feelings or memories, enjoy jokes, and even monitor the other person's emotions. All this happens while we effortlessly unravel the meaning of what they're saying. Feats like this are well beyond the ability of any existing computer system.

◁ **Despite appearances to an** outside observer, the operator in this room does not understand Chinese. This imaginary test shows how difficult it is to know if "intelligent machines" really understand things.

SEE ALSO

The information age	9
Thinking machines	10–11
Thinking power	70–71

Why can't science help us **live forever?**

Although many of us will live longer than our ancestors, the general human life span has never changed. Healthy living can lower the risk of getting certain diseases, and medicine can help us to beat some of them, but so far, no one has found a way to halt the process of aging and eventual death.

△ **While a few scientists are** looking at the possibilities of stopping the aging process, many more are searching for ways to beat disease and give people a healthy and active old age.

❓ How does a body change when it gets old?

Wrinkles, sagging skin, and gray hair are the hallmarks of old age—but these are just the things you can see on the outside. As you age, your bones become more brittle and the moving parts of your body wear out. These changes happen because many of the body's cells can no longer repair and replace themselves. Cells change like this because the genes inside them develop random faults over time. This deterioration stops the body from working properly.

▽ **Wrinkles develop** as aging skin loses an ingredient called elastin.

❓ How will society change if we all live longer?

If more people have longer lives, it will become increasingly important to cater for older people in areas such as work, healthcare, entertainment, and technology. For example, older people need more medical attention, so an aging society will need to spend more on its healthcare system. This is already beginning to happen as the number of older, active people rises. Of course, older people have many years of experience, so society can benefit greatly from their wisdom.

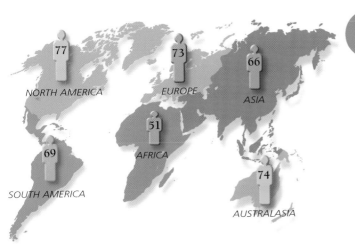

△ The average human life expectancy varies from continent to continent.

NORTH AMERICA — 77
EUROPE — 73
ASIA — 66
AFRICA — 51
SOUTH AMERICA — 69
AUSTRALASIA — 74

? How can we increase our life span?

Medical science already helps more people to live longer. Without treatment for serious injuries, illnesses, or infections, many of us would already be dead. We may not know how to halt aging, but we can all increase our chances of a long, healthy life. Your life expectancy increases if you avoid smoking, take good care of your body, exercise a little, and eat a balanced diet. Sadly, not everyone around the world has the same opportunity to live like this. Improving access to good food and healthcare around the world would help many more people to live longer.

? Why do we all eventually die?

The longer you live, the more likely you are to develop heart problems, cancer, or other diseases. Anything like this has the potential to kill you. Even if you are lucky enough to stay free from disease, your body can't go on forever. Eventually, your deteriorating cells will stop a vital part of your body from working. This will lead to your death. Cell deterioration puts a limit on the human life span—so far, no one has lived for more than 130 years. Of course, there are important, natural reasons why we all eventually need to die. Imagine how difficult it would be for humans to survive if for every active, young person, there were dozens of old and infirm people.

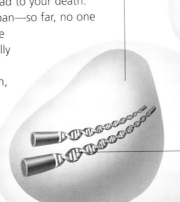

Old human cell

Cell nucleus

Young human cell

Double helix

Telomeres fray

Telomeres

△ The genes in your cells are arranged in chains called chromosomes. The ends of your chromosomes, known as telomeres, fray throughout your life. Telomeres act like body clocks—the more they fray, the more your body ages.

△ Dolly the clone (see page 15) had second-hand genes. Will she grow old too early?

? Have scientists found ways to "stop the clock"?

Although scientists have identified the body changes that make us grow old, they don't know how to halt them. Aging could be stopped if we could help cells to stay alive—but this could also be very dangerous. Cells in your body are given a limited life span so that they die before their genes develop faults. When you are young, your body replaces dead cells with new ones in perfect condition. Old cells may develop faults that could trigger cancers.

SEE ALSO

The new genetics	14–15
Cryogenic scientist	58–59
Genetics breakthroughs	74–75

Are we alone in the **universe?**

△ Anyone with a computer connected to the Internet can help in the search for extraterrestrials. SETI researchers link up computers around the world and borrow their calculating power when they're not in use.

No one knows if there is life outside Earth—but it's a question that many space scientists take seriously. For over 40 years, they have been sweeping the sky for radio signals from intelligent life on other planets. Work of this kind is called SETI (the Search for Extraterrestrial Intelligence). The largest SETI project is Project Phoenix, run by an independent team of scientists.

? How are scientists looking for extraterrestrials?

As there don't seem to be any extraterrestrials sharing the solar system with us, SETI teams search much farther afield. Very slowly, they are sweeping the skies, looking for stars that are surrounded by planets. There is a chance that one of these planets may have the right atmosphere and temperature to sustain life, just like on Earth. The SETI scientists are looking for radio signals coming from these stars—artificial signals from machines made by extraterrestrials. They use powerful computers to cut out the background hiss—radio waves that are produced naturally by stars. They are also careful to ignore any radio signals that come from Earth for TV, radio, and air traffic control.

△ Scientists use some of the largest radio telescopes on the planet to search for signs of extraterrestrial life.

Io

What are the chances of finding life on another planet?

There are countless billions of stars in the universe. From investigations with telescopes, we know that many of them are surrounded by planets. The chances that a few of these planets contain life is fairly high. But the likelihood that we could meet up with this life is much lower. It would be impractical to mount a mission in search of aliens. Even using a lightsail (see page 23), a trip around the hundred nearest stars would take millions of years. That's why scientists look for signals from aliens instead.

◁ ▷ A planet (left) orbits a pair of stars in a distant galaxy. Io (right) is a lifeless moon of Jupiter in our own solar system. A planet or moon could be a cradle for extraterrestrial life.

▷ This message to the rest of the universe was put inside the *Pioneer 10* probe, which drifted out of the solar system on June 13, 1983. It shows the location of Earth, how humans look, and the way we pick up radio signals. The disk (right) contains a recording of sounds of life on Earth.

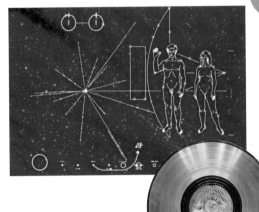

How easy would it be for extraterrestrials to get in touch?

It's quite easy to make a radio signal that can go a long way through space—our TV and radio broadcasts do this all the time. But the chances of getting a signal picked up are slim. Extraterrestrials could have been calling Earth any time over the last 10 billion years, after the first planets formed. But humans have known about radio for only a century. Before then, any radio calls to Earth would have been ignored.

Has there been any evidence of extraterrestrial life ?

So far, we haven't found any alien life, but there have been many false alarms. One of the most famous concerned a radio signal picked up in Ohio. It looked so much like a message from another solar system that the researcher who found it scribbled the word "Wow" across it when he printed out its data. Because the signal was never picked up again, it was written off as an error—but the origin of the "Wow" signal remains a mystery.

◁ This robot visited Mars in 1998. One of its tasks was to look for fossil evidence of former Martian life.

Are
we still **evolving?**

Like all other life on the planet, we evolved from other creatures over millions of years. We share our ancestors with modern apes. As far as we know, humans are the most intelligent creatures that live on planet Earth—but when the first *Homo sapiens* (modern humans) appeared around a million years ago (mya), the process of evolution didn't stop. Humans, along with all other living things, continue to evolve. It's fascinating to wonder how evolution will change us in the future.

? What changes on Earth could be shaping our evolution?

In the 5 million years it has taken us to evolve from apelike ancestors, the Earth's climate has changed, influencing human evolution. It's likely that *Homo habilis* emerged from *Australopithecus* around 3.5 million years ago, when the climate in Africa became much cooler and drier. Of course, Earth's climate is still changing. Shelter, clothing, medicine, and other human inventions make us more resilient to gradual climate changes. But a sudden change in climate could kill many humans— and other animals—and send evolution on a different course.

▷ **The bones of this hominid,** who died around 2.5 million years ago, were discovered in South Africa. We could be her direct descendants.

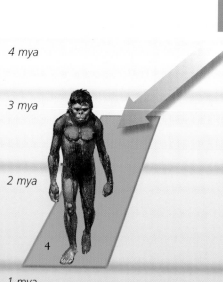

4 mya

3 mya

2 mya

1 mya

4

△ **Homo sapiens is just one of many** species that evolved from our apelike ancestors. Paleontologists (people who study ancient life) compare the hominids (humanlike creatures) that have existed over the last 5 million years. They are trying to work out our human family tree.

KEY TO EVOLUTIONARY TREE
1 *Australopithicene*
2 *Australopithecus bahrelghazali*
3 *Australopithecus africanus*
4 *Australopithecus boisei*
5 *Homo habilis*
6 *Homo erectus*
7 *Homo sapiens*

◁ A Paris street at the end of the 19th century (left) and the end of the 20th century (below).

◁ In only 100 years, our city streets have changed dramatically. Modern humans have to survive in very different surroundings from their ancestors. How will we evolve to suit our new habitats?

What are the most likely ways we will evolve?

No one can be certain how humans will evolve in the future, but we can look at how the things we do may alter the course of our evolution.
One example is the invention of the automobile. Thousands of years ago, families who were good hunters were the most likely to survive. However, survival in a modern town or city depends more on good road sense. If cars are around for thousands of years more, the characteristics that make us skillful at crossing roads are likely to become stronger! We're still not sure if inventions like the car will alter the course of evolution. Some people think these inventions won't survive long enough to have any effect at all.

How soon are we likely to see changes?

Evolution is usually a very slow process. Around a quarter of a million generations of hominids separate you from your apelike ancestors. But some scientists think new technology will make evolution happen much faster. Very soon, for example, a type of genetic medicine, called human germline therapy (see page 40), could become a reality. In theory, it would enable us to change human traits, by altering the genes of human embryos, in a single generation.

Can science change the pattern of human evolution?

It's possible that some human discoveries and inventions have already changed the course of evolution. Inventions such as the supermarket, for example, have changed the skills we need to survive. And medicine has helped many more of us to survive. This means it has a big impact on future humankind. Germline therapy (see page 40) has the potential to alter humans, gene by gene. Perhaps this, rather than natural evolution, will be the process that changes us in the future. Meanwhile, some scientists are wondering if humans will evolve alongside thinking machines. Future humans could plug themselves into machines to replace ailing or aging bodies. Smart machines could also enhance the human brain.

◁ A few scientists imagine that future humans will plug their minds and bodies into computers, creating a new form of life.

How
and when will our **world die?**

We live in a solar system of nine planets that orbit a single star, the Sun. Our solar system has existed for only 5 billion years or so, and it won't be here for ever. Scattered around the universe, we can see the remains of many stars that have run out of fuel. Just like any other star, the Sun will eventually meet the same fate. Will Earth still be here when the Sun dies or will an earlier catastrophe have destroyed it? Will humans—or any other species—be around to witness the death of our home planet?

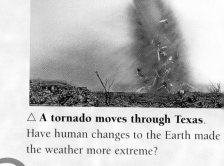

△ **A tornado moves through Texas.** Have human changes to the Earth made the weather more extreme?

?How do humans affect the long-term future of the Earth?

As we have found ways to use the Earth's crops, oceans, fossil fuels, and other resources, we have changed the planet we live on. However, people are unsure how some of these changes will affect the long-term future of the Earth. Are we making the world warmer (see pages 32–33), or is global warming part of the Earth's natural cycle of change? Will humans actually help the Earth survive longer? For example, will we build a system that can protect the Earth from large, incoming asteroids?

▷ **Taken in the wilderness of Tunguska, Siberia, this photograph shows the devastation caused by a small asteroid collision in June 1908.**

?How is the Earth likely to end?

Although only a remote possibility, a sudden, huge change in the Earth's climate is the most likely cause of its destruction. This could be triggered by millions of tons of dust thrown into the atmosphere. The dust could come from a giant asteroid hitting Earth or a mighty volcanic eruption. Humans could generate a deadly amount of dust in a nuclear war. The dust would block out the Sun, plunging Earth into a very long, dark, and deadly winter.

▷ **Space scientists estimate there's only a one in 10,000 chance of Earth colliding with a giant asteroid in the next century.**

? Will the Sun outlive the Earth?

When the Sun dies, the Earth will die with it. Our middle-aged Sun has been burning for around 5 billion years. In another 5 billion years or so, it will run out of fuel and disappear in a puff of heat. It will become a red giant that will swell to many times its present size, engulfing the Earth and the rest of the solar system. You will have died long before this happens—and so may the rest of life on Earth.

▷ This photograph captures a supernova in action (see below). Our Sun isn't heavy enough to end in an explosion like this.

▷ Lighter stars, such as our Sun, fade away as red giants (top). A heavy star (bottom) dies in a spectacular blast called a supernova.

Red giant

Lighter star

Gas and dust from giant stars and explosions mix with interstellar clouds where new stars are born

Heavy star

Supernova

? How will the universe end?

Scientists don't know if the universe will end with a bang or a whimper. Its fate depends on the total mass of the stars, planets, dust clouds, and everything else it contains—something that scientists don't agree on. If we live in a heavy universe, the forces of gravity will eventually stop it expanding and cooling. It will shrink back to a singularity (see page 39) in a reverse of the Big Bang, known as the Big Crunch. A lighter universe will never stop expanding. But as it grows cooler, its stars will die and any activity will slowly fade away.

◁ This galaxy, Andromeda, will collide with our own, the Milky Way, in about 3.5 billion years time.

? What are the chances of a deadly collision?

Earth is always being bombarded by asteroids and other objects in space—but the chances of a collision destroying Earth are very low. Even if we avoid any other impacts, in 3.5 billion years or so our galaxy will bump into its neighbor, Andromeda. Our galaxy could glide through Andromeda without hitting other stars, or the solar system could be destroyed in a deadly collision. It's not worth losing any sleep over this—you'll be gone long before these two galaxies meet! By then, the Earth itself may have disappeared.

What are the biggest unanswered questions?

△ **Perhaps mini Big Bangs could make new universes spring from our own. This could explain how a multiverse is created (see pages 36–37).**

As fast as scientists make new discoveries about the universe, they raise new questions. Some of the biggest mysteries concern the origin of the universe and the events that happened just after the Big Bang. If you find these mysteries puzzling, you are not alone. They are also challenging some of the greatest scientists at work today.

? What happened just after the Big Bang?

Most cosmologists (space scientists) think our universe began with a Big Bang (see page 39). But they still aren't sure how every part of the growing universe expanded, with perfect timing, to make the kind of universe we live in today. A new version of the Big Bang theory attempts to answer this puzzle. It says the universe had lots of random, mini Big Bangs in its first fraction of a billionth of a second, which made it grow rapidly.

? What is the empty space between the stars?

Amazingly, the black space between the stars isn't empty at all. Even if you remove all the scraps of gas and dust, something is left behind. Scientists are still trying to puzzle out what this is. Some of it could be particles that exist for just a fleeting moment. Called virtual particles, they carry forces around the universe (see pages 20–21).

? Where is most of the universe hiding?

Something invisible is helping to hold the universe together. Gravity pulls together any two things that have mass (are more than zero ounces). It forces the stars, planets, gas clouds, and other parts of the universe toward each other—but this isn't enough to create all the force that's needed to keep the universe together. The universe must have an invisible, extra ingredient that creates a bigger force of gravity. Scientists call this mysterious missing ingredient dark matter.

◁ **Scientists lay a dark matter detector at the bottom of a salt mine to shield it from stray particles from space, called cosmic rays. Dark matter could make up nine-tenths of the mass of the universe.**

JOBFILE

Jobfile

JOB TITLE:

Vulcanologist

JOB DESCRIPTION:

David Cooper, a vulcanologist, researches lava flows and looks for ways to predict the hazards that are caused by volcanic eruptions. David was near the Kilauea volcano when we met him. Sheltered in a concrete hut, his team was comparing notes after a long day taking measurements on the local lava flows.

NAME AND AGE:

*Dr. David Cooper, 40

*"Dr. David Cooper" is a fictional character

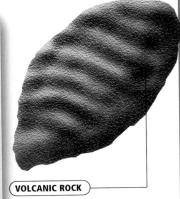

VOLCANIC ROCK

Many vulcanologists investigate the debris of past eruptions. It is rich in unusual minerals and ores.

This volcano looks quite peaceful—is this where you do most work?

Don't be taken in by appearances! Kilauea may not seem to be up to much now, but it's one of the most active volcanoes in Hawaii. In fact, it's actually erupting as we speak. It may not look all that dramatic from here, but it's been spewing lava (molten rock) continuously for almost 20 years. Some parts of the volcano have been completely scorched. They're far too dangerous for an overnight stay.

Do you worry about your safety?

Of course, in the back of our minds, I suppose we all do. As far as anxiety goes, being a vulcanologist works both ways. On the one hand, I feel that I have enough experience of volcanoes to know when I should feel safe. I've been studying the volcano behind me for most of my career, and I know the signs that mean we're heading for trouble. To me, Kilauea is like a friend who always has a bubbling temper—and hopefully I can tell when it is about to flare up into an unpleasant outburst! On the other hand, as an experienced volcano watcher, I've developed a healthy respect for these beasts. In fact, I sometimes get anxious because I know exactly what they can do. I've had to advise villagers whose homes, farms, and livestock have been destroyed, without warning, by volcanic action. Imagine having all your possessions swept away, just like that.

MEASURING ACTIVITY

A scientist on the flank of an active volcano pushes a flow meter into open cracks in the rocks. The hot, smelly lava is flowing out of vents that come from the core of the volcano, deep under the Earth. Vulcanologists can rarely find out what they need to know just by working in the laboratory. They have to get close to the active volcanoes themselves. This scientist will use her figures to estimate how much lava is flowing through the vent.

What have you done today?

Well, we were meant to go on the flanks of the volcano to measure the viscosity (thickness) of the lava flows. But we spotted some fascinating fissures—cracks in the rocks. These have appeared only in the last few days, and they have destroyed our old measuring site. But we all agreed they were amazing to look at, and we couldn't take our eyes off them. They were making their way across fresh ground as we watched. When you see a volcano crack open the rocks before your eyes, it can make you feel very humble.

BLACK SMOKER

Volcanoes are scattered all over the Earth, even under the sea. This photograph shows a "black smoker," an undersea volcano that belches dark smoke into the water more than 5,000 feet below the ocean surface.

ERUPTION

The moment that Mount St. Helens blew up in Washington in 1980. Vulcanologists dream of seeing the beginning of an eruption, but volcanoes are very unpredictable and the chances of being in the right place as one goes into action are remote.

SATELLITE IMAGING

A satellite captured this stunning view of a volcano in action. The ash from an eruption can quickly spread, blocking out the Sun's rays. Larger volcanoes throw enough debris into the atmosphere to lower the Earth's temperature.

You clearly love volcanoes— but how did you get hooked?

Well, you may not believe it looking at me today, but I originally wanted to be an astronaut. I was about 12 when Skylab was developed. You may not remember it. Skylab was America's first space station, launched in 1973. I recall having dozens of books and magazines about that thing. I had posters of it plastered all over my bedroom

he debris scattered across the landscape by a
volcano is rich in minerals and ores. Volcanic ash
fertilizes the soil, helping new life to grow. In this
way, after destroying the surrounding habitat, a
volcano helps new life to flourish.

TOTAL DESTRUCTION

This scene of devastation is on the flank of
Mount St. Helens, just a few weeks after the
1980 eruption. Trees and wildlife have been totally
destroyed. Most geological events take thousands
of years to alter the face of the Earth, but a
volcano can completely transform the landscape
in a single day.

VOLCANO MONITORING

Two vulcanologists edge closer to the rim of a
crater to take measurements of a volcano in action.
They are wearing face masks to protect their lungs
from the ash- and fume-laden air. An active
volcano can generate enough ash to cause a
"white out." When this happens, vulcanologists
need a flashlight to find their way back to camp.

walls. Skylab got me excited about
venturing into space. One evening,
though, when I was watching TV,
there was a special feature on the
work that future astronauts would
do. At the time, there was talk of
sending people to Mars, some time
in the future, to study the rocks for
signs of life. One of the astronauts
on this trip would have to be a
geologist, someone who could
make sense of the rocks. From the
moment I heard this, I was
convinced geology would be my
passport into space.

What happened to those plans?

If NASA gave me a call to join
them on a space mission, I'd be
there tomorrow. But space science
has moved on a lot since the day I
saw that report. Scientists have
already been back to Mars—but
they sent a roving robot, the Mars
Explorer, instead of a person. The
robot was controlled by experts
back on Earth, which made a lot
of sense. Of course, my life has
moved on a lot since then, too.
While I was studying geology at
college, I joined a team researching
volcanoes. In 1980, we went to
monitor the aftermath of the
Mount St. Helen's eruption, in
Washington state. Visiting the site
so soon after the mountain had
exploded was unbelievable.
Everything was covered in white
volcanic ash. The place was
completely silent because so much
wildlife had perished. The air was
thick with a sulfurous smell. As I
picked my way around the site,
I realized I had reached the alien
landscape that had always been
in my dreams.

So, what do vulcanologists actually do?

My team is interested in measuring
volcanoes while they're in action. If
we can learn more about lava and
the way that it flows, we can
improve our ability to predict the
hazards when an eruption
happens. Other vulcanologists are
into different things. Some friends
back at college, for example, are
finding better ways to tap hot
volcanic rocks to make geothermal
power plants.

What's your greatest ambition?

To fly over a volcano the moment
an eruption begins. I only know of
one other colleague who's been
lucky enough to catch an eruption
in its first few moments. If I got
the chance to see one start, I think
I'd forget any terror for a few
moments while I sat back and
watched the show!

JOB TITLE:

Archaeologist

JOB DESCRIPTION:

Dr. Susan Wyatt is an archaeologist, a scientist who studies the things left behind by people that lived in the past. Recently, Susan has been looking at the remains of a rare Roman burial site, discovered by accident under the streets of London, England.

NAME AND AGE:

*Dr. Susan Wyatt, 29

* "Dr. Susan Wyatt" is a fictional character

TOOLS FOR THE JOB

Susan uses picks and trowels to dig—but as soon as she gets close to a specimen, she removes any mud and soil very carefully since it may contain vital fragments. Susan uses a tape measure to record the position of any artifacts she finds.

Do you dig for buried treasure?

Hardly ever! As an archaeologist, I'm interested in far more than precious jewelry and coins. Imagine a group of archaeologists, hundreds of years in the future, who are trying to piece together a picture of your life just from the objects you left behind. The contents of your trash can would tell them more about your daily life—what you ate, where you shopped, the newspapers or comics you read—than what's inside any jewelry box. So I spend most of my time sifting through ancient garbage dumps.

How old are the sites you study?

I'm mainly interested in the Romans who lived in London around 1,600 years ago, but many of my colleagues deal with the city's more recent history. A few look at buildings and objects that were used only a couple of centuries ago. Once you have training in archaeology, you can apply your skills to any period— you could even use them to sift through last year's trash!

How often do you make an interesting find?

I can work for many months sifting through broken jugs and bottles, Roman coins, and other predictable odds and ends that surface in the city. Occasionally, though, a colleague hits the jackpot, and my working life will be turned upside-down. This happened just four months ago when someone in my office

AT THE SITE

This photo shows an exciting find in London— a complete Roman sarcophagus (tomb). The objects found on a dig are treated like evidence at a crime scene. Susan and her colleagues are careful not to damage or disturb them.

A CLOSER LOOK

The sarcophagus is opened to reveal the decorated lid of a coffin.

received a phone call from a building company. One of the workmen operating a digger had come across some human remains. We went over there immediately and spent the next four months using every hour of daylight to uncover as much of the site as possible.

Whose body was it?

That wasn't a question we could answer immediately. However, after we pieced the site together again, we found it was the body of a Roman boy. We were fascinated to discover he was one of many Roman burials in the area. We'd stumbled on a burial site that must have been outside the ancient city walls around 16 centuries ago.

What tools do you need to be an archaeologist?

On a basic level, we use picks and trowels to move large amounts of earth. Of course, I need something more high-tech to analyze samples from objects that have been found. You may have heard of carbon dating—this is one test I use to judge the age of my specimens. I look at the way the carbon atoms in a specimen have decayed over centuries to calculate the age of the object. X-rays and microscopes let me examine any layers of paint that have been applied to an

GRAVE GOODS

Objects placed in ancient graves give us clues about the people who were buried in them. Near the London sarcophagus was a glass container (above), used to carry expensive perfume. This find suggests the buried woman was very wealthy.

object. A machine called a mass spectrometer helps me to identify the chemicals in fragments such as a shard of glass or a piece of pottery. All of these technologies give me clues that I can then use to piece together the story of the people who used the objects we discovered. If I know the impurities in a glass fragment, for example, I may be able to tell the quality of the glass and its origin. As an archaeologist, you have to be a little bit of everything—a scientist, a detective, and a historian. But the most important tool for any one of us is the human mind.

RARE FIND

When London archaeologists opened the Roman sarcophagus on the left, they were surprised to find that it contained an intact lead coffin. In the laboratory, they opened the coffin to discover the body of a young woman who had died when she was about 23 years old. Remains as complete as this are rare.

JOB TITLE:

Cryogenic scientist

JOB DESCRIPTION:

Jenny Fischer researches cryogenics—the science of ultracold temperatures. It was a warm summer's afternoon when we met her at the cryogenics lab. As we sipped cool drinks, she talked about her investigations into some of the coldest temperatures that can exist in the universe.

* "Dr. Jenny Fischer" is a fictional character

NAME AND AGE:

*Dr. Jenny Fischer, 35

SUPERCONDUCTORS

Superconductors need to be ultracold. Even so-called high temperature superconductors only work if they're at least—150° F. The coolants needed to keep things this cold are very expensive. Jenny is one of many scientists searching for ways to make superconductors that work in higher temperatures. Superconductors like these could then be be put into more widespread use.

How cold is ultracold?

Well, today the air temperature must be about 85° F. But imagine yourself transported to Siberia, one of the coldest parts of the world, on the coldest day ever recorded. The air temperature is around 125 degrees below zero. In other words, it's dropped by almost 200 degrees. If I left this cup of coffee on the window ledge, it would be frozen solid in a minute.

NITROGEN

Jenny uses nitrogen to keep her cryogenic samples cold. Nitrogen makes up around four-fifths of the air we breathe. In normal room conditions, nitrogen is a gas, but when it is cooled to at least −320° F, it becomes a liquid.

Is this the temperature you are interested in?

Believe it or not, I actually work with things that are far colder! Imagine dropping the temperature by 200 degrees twice over. You'd be talking about a temperature of around −350° F. At this temperature, the air itself would turn to liquid. Well, I'm working at a temperature up to 100 degrees cooler even than this.

BRAIN SCAN

Showing structures inside the brain, this MRI scan was produced by detecting the body's faint magnetism. MRI scanners that use superconductors would show far more detail. They can detect magnetism 100 billion times weaker than the Earth's magnetic field.

Wow! But why does anyone need to be this cold?

We'd certainly die in temperatures this cold—but they're fascinating to investigate. I became curious about them as a physics student, when I learned that they existed all over our universe. Did you know that whenever you look at the dark space between the stars, you're looking at something that's −450° F? Not surprising really, when you think it's been cooling steadily since the Big Bang around 15 billion years ago.

How do things change at ultracold temperatures?

I suppose the strangest thing of all is what happens to certain materials, such as the alloy

ULTRACOLD

Things have heat because the atoms inside them are in constant, microscopic motion. In general, as materials cool, their atoms move less energetically. This is why coldness has a limit. At a temperature called absolute zero, atoms can't move with less energy. They have reached the coldest temperature that can exist. Absolute zero is around −459° F.

ULTRACOLD TEMPERATURES	
32° F	Water freezes
−126° F	Coldest recorded air temperature
−320° F	Nitrogen in the air becomes liquid
−452.1° F	Helium in the air becomes liquid
−454° F	Temperature of empty space between stars
−459.67° F	Absolute zero

MAGLEV

Engineers have been using superconductors to revive a form of transportation that was abandoned in the 1970s. Called Maglev, it uses magnets to levitate (raise) a train above its tracks, giving a smooth, silent ride. Superconductors make extremely powerful, tiny magnets—perfect levitating materials for the new Maglev trains.

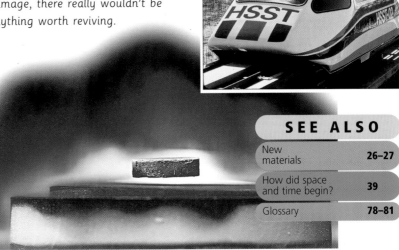

vanadium-silicon. They become perfect conductors of electricity—superconductors. Because of their properties, they also make tiny, powerful magnets. I suppose the most exciting thing about these materials is what you can do with them. Using superconductors, we have a way to revolutionize medical imaging, computing, and transportation. We could build more sensitive scanners, more powerful computers, and smoother, more efficient trains.

Do you freeze people?

No! If you watch science fiction films, you might think that people can be frozen for years—centuries even—then magically brought back to life. It's a very attractive idea—but I'm afraid it's nonsense. You see, when

you freeze a human body, even by just a few degrees, the water in the body expands as it forms little ice crystals. As they grow, these crystals cut through the tissue of the body like razors. Sure, you could "defrost" a frozen body centuries in the future. But you'd be faced with so much cell damage, there really wouldn't be anything worth reviving.

JOB TITLE:

Telesurgeon

JOB DESCRIPTION:

Patrick Odimayo is a "telesurgeon," a doctor who uses computers and robotics to help patients in remote locations, without actually visiting them himself. Patrick showed us around his workplace and told us how telesurgery works.

NAME AND AGE:

*Dr. Patrick Odimayo, 35

* "Dr. Patrick Odimayo" is a fictional character

SEE ALSO

The information age	9
Thinking machines	10–11
Glossary	78–81

Telesurgery sounds very sci-fi? Can it really be done?

Well, yes, I'm already doing it myself, in a limited way. This morning, for example, I saw an elderly female patient over the Internet. She was suffering from a rare gallbladder problem that had flared up suddenly, and she was in a great deal of pain. The problem was that she lived in a remote fishing community in Scotland, on an island many miles away from suitable specialized care. In years gone by, this woman would have needed to make a long and uncomfortable trip to a specialized hospital where surgeons could give her the treatment she needed. But thanks to the Internet, I was able to examine the patient in her local operating room, close to her home. My computer was attached to an endoscope—a tiny camera that can go inside the body— allowing me to see live pictures over the Internet. I looked at the pictures at 10:30 this morning, and by 10:40 I'd made a phone call to a surgeon in Scotland, telling him the best way to treat this patient's problem.

Could you perform surgery over the Internet?

I wouldn't be confident yet about controlling a scalpel on-line (using an Internet link). Even using a special phone line, the system would be far too slow and unreliable to put a patient's life at stake. However, I'm part of a team at this hospital that is trying to make on-line surgery practical. We're working with a large computer company to

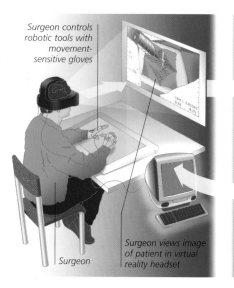

Surgeon controls robotic tools with movement-sensitive gloves

Surgeon views image of patient in virtual reality headset

Surgeon

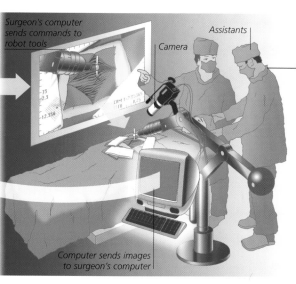

Surgeon's computer sends commands to robot tools

Camera

Assistants

Computer sends images to surgeon's computer

HOW IT WILL WORK

The patient will be given an anesthetic and put in an operating room. Robotic tools, scanners, and cameras around the patient will be linked, over the Internet, to a remote computer. This could be in the next room— or on a different continent. To operate on the patient, Patrick will watch images on this computer and use machines to control the robotic tools.

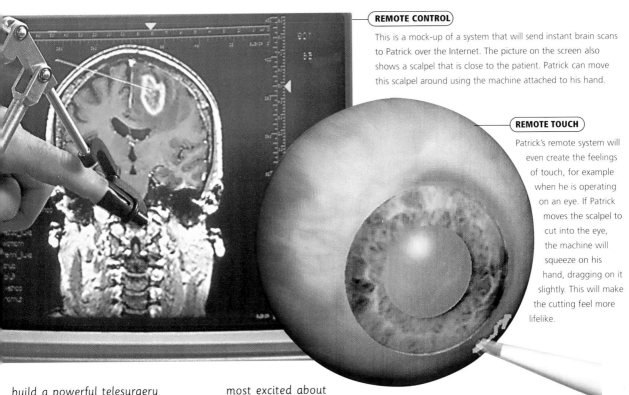

This is a mock-up of a system that will send instant brain scans to Patrick over the Internet. The picture on the screen also shows a scalpel that is close to the patient. Patrick can move this scalpel around using the machine attached to his hand.

REMOTE TOUCH

Patrick's remote system will even create the feelings of touch, for example when he is operating on an eye. If Patrick moves the scalpel to cut into the eye, the machine will squeeze on his hand, dragging on it slightly. This will make the cutting feel more lifelike.

build a powerful telesurgery system. Eventually, this system will let surgeons see, feel, and control scalpels, cameras, and other equipment that are thousands of miles away.

Why don't we train more surgeons instead?

It's an appealing idea, but no matter how many surgeons there are, there will always be some groups of people without access to emergency surgery. Personally, I'm

most excited about telesurgery that can help groups of astronauts on board future space missions. An in-flight tele-operating room could give them access to the best treatment on planet Earth.

REMOTE VISITS

Some of the technology used in telesurgery has already been tried and tested in other settings. Robots linked to video cameras have been used to control tools and visit sites remotely under the oceans (left) or on the planet Mars (above).

What's the most sophisticated telesurgery equipment around?

Mmm, that's an interesting question. You may think our remote-controlled cutting tools are impressive. Although they are only prototypes, they already allow me to do finely controlled work. However, these machines have one big drawback. They can't adapt and make decisions independently. They're only as good as the telesurgeons who are controlling them. Fortunately, I don't do telesurgery alone. There is always a skilled assistant at the other end of the Internet link, checking the tools are working well and warning me if anything is going wrong. I'd single out my human colleague as the most sophisticated part of the set-up. Even if he or she is not an expert, the skills of a human being can still surpass those of any machine.

JOB TITLE:

Formula 1 engineer

JOB DESCRIPTION:

Colin Fury designs and tests the latest Formula 1 racing cars. We met Colin at the test track and asked him how he'd found his way into such a glamorous industry. Colin shared his passion for Formula 1 and explained how a training in aeronautics had helped him to get involved.

NAME AND AGE:

*Colin Fury, 41

* "Colin Fury" is a fictional character

FIREPROOF SUIT

Almost every branch of engineering is represented in the biggest Formula 1 teams. Some of Colin's team mates are materials scientists who design fireproof suits for the drivers.

When did you get into Formula 1?

As a kid, I'd always loved watching Grand Prix on TV, but my real passion was for aircraft. It wasn't until I was in my twenties that I became gripped by the Formula 1 bug. I was working for a big aircraft company at the time, designing wings for their new passenger aircraft. You see, I trained as an aeronautical engineer. I had actually wanted to fly, but decided to go into engineering when I discovered that I was too tall for the air force.

How did you move from aeronautics to racing cars?

I remember working in the company's huge wind tunnels—laboratories where giant fans make air move at high speed. When the fast-moving air flows over aircraft wings in the wind tunnel, the wings have to cope with the same stresses and strains as they would when the aircraft is really flying. We'd put our latest designs in these tunnels and track the passage of air to see how the wings were performing. But as you can imagine, these wind tunnels are very expensive

bits of kit. To make a profit, the company hired them out to other researchers and used them around the clock. One evening, when I was working late, I bumped into a few people who were starting an evening shift. They were Formula 1 engineers who had booked the wind tunnel to track the passage of air over their latest car body. I watched them at work for a while, then had a long chat with them. By the end of the evening, I was completely hooked.

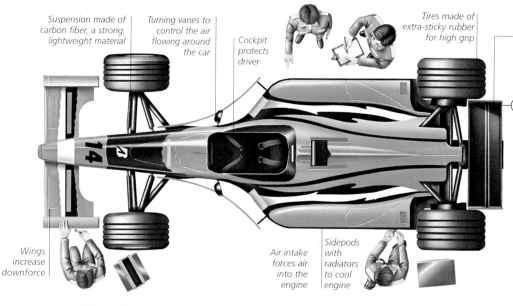

Suspension made of carbon fiber, a strong, lightweight material

Turning vanes to control the air flowing around the car

Cockpit protects driver

Tires made of extra-sticky rubber for high grip

Wings increase downforce

Wings increase downforce

Air intake forces air into the engine

Sidepods with radiators to cool engine

FORMULA 1 CAR

A Formula 1 engine turns five times faster than a road car engine. This gives it a characteristic, high-pitched scream. Its body is designed to allow it to grip the road and enable it to cut through the air as cleanly as possible. This lets it corner sharply and drive at high speed. Every part of the car can be replaced and adjusted very quickly.

READOUT
Computer circuitry tells the driver the car's speed and performance. A radio transmitter also beams this data back to engineers in the pit.

Was it easy to make the shift from one to the other?

Luckily, at the time it was. In fact, most engineers concerned with Formula 1 aerodynamics started off in the aircraft industry. A good training in engineering can open up doors almost anywhere.

What interested you?

These engineers were grappling with the same problems as me— how to make machines that will move swiftly and efficiently through the air. But their work seemed much more exciting because they were working to the most incredible deadlines. They had to use all their skill, flair, and imagination to come up with a new car design every year. I was involved in aircraft designs that could take up to 15 years to complete—but they made a new car every season.

HELMET DESIGN

In Formula 1, even the driver's seating position and helmet design are developed with aerodynamics in mind.

How do you spend your time?

Most of the year is spent designing the new car, using computer simulations. We do all our number-crunching on a supercomputer called the SPARC Station. Using a computer-aided design (CAD) package, we draw dozens of versions of the car before we even attempt to make a real prototype. Once we've built a real-life model, we spend a couple of months testing our latest model in the wind tunnel before bringing it out on the test track.

SEE ALSO

DOWNFORCE GRIP

Colin makes sure that air flowing over the wings and other parts of this Formula 1 car give it as much downforce as possible. This is the force that makes the car grip the road. A fast-moving Formula 1 car grips surfaces so well, it could ride along the ceiling!

Do you still enjoy watching Formula 1?

Yes—but I have to admit I focus on the tiny details of the car more than I used to! For instance, I've been known to freeze-frame the video player to take a closer look at the rear wing. Even a simple-looking part like this has been painstakingly angled and curved to give the car as much downforce as possible. Downforce gives the car grip so it can move quickly.

What's the formula for a perfect car?

A racing car is very different from an ordinary car. Your average car is bulky and designed to work for years. A racing car, however, needs to work perfectly on the track, but not carry any unnecessary fuel or parts. It's been said that the perfect Formula 1 car would fall apart as soon as it crossed the winning line!

What about getting behind the wheel?

Not likely! I'm too tall to be a pilot, so I'd never squeeze into the cockpit of a racing car. Also, I'm a bit too old to get started in Formula 1. If you talk to all the best drivers, they got involved in the sport as teenagers, usually honing their skills in go-cart racing. I don't think I'd be up for the training regime either. When you see a driver in a Formula 1 car, you may not realize that he or she is an athlete. To a spectator, it looks like the car is doing all the work. You may be surprised to know that the drivers have to work out, like any other sportsmen and women, to develop the muscles they need to cope with the car. You see, Formula 1 cars corner so fast, drivers can experience accelerations of up to 3G—in other words, their head feels three times as heavy as normal. You should see the exercises they have to do, lifting weights with their neck, to get fit enough to drive.

FACTFILE

Factfile

The building blocks of matter

The atom

Every substance around you is made of tiny particles, called atoms. Each atom is so tiny that several million of them would stretch across the period at the end of this sentence. The characteristics of these tiny scraps of matter and the way they join together help to determine the properties of any material. Until the beginning of the 20th century, most scientists thought the atom could never be broken apart. They believed that it was the smallest building block of matter. However, in the years that followed, as people studied matter and energy more closely than ever, they gradually changed this view. Experiments have shown that the atom is itself made up of even smaller units, which we call subatomic particles.

▷ The haze in this picture is the blur left behind by the electrons circling the nucleus. The darkest areas of the haze show the areas where electrons go most often.

Electrons

Proton

Neutron

Inside an atom

As they studied subatomic particles, scientists developed their understanding of how these particles combined to make an atom. Until about 80 years ago, many scientists thought that electrons moved around the outside of an atom in a regular way, just like clockwork. We now know they flit randomly, following paths that can never be exactly predicted. Scientists use probability to understand how subatomic particles behave. Probability is a branch of mathematics that studies the chances of events happening. The picture on this page shows the way most scientists view the atom today.

▽ Every proton and neutron is itself made up of three smaller particles, called quarks.

Quarks

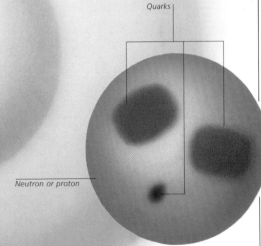

Neutron or proton

Electrons

Tiny, lightweight particles, called electrons, flit randomly around the dense nucleus of an atom. These particles carry a negative electric charge. In some situations, electrons can flow through a substance by moving from atom to atom. When they do this, they create an electric current. At present, scientists do not think that the electron is made up of smaller particles. The electron seems to be a fundamental particle of the universe.

Protons and neutrons

The nucleus of an atom is made of protons and neutrons, particles that are many times heavier than an electron. The proton carries a positive electric charge, but the neutron carries no charge at all. Protons and neutrons are themselves made up of even smaller particles, called quarks. Three quarks make up a single proton or neutron. The forces between them bind the protons and neutrons together and enable them to pack together tightly within an atomic nucleus.

Atomic structures

The pictures on this page show how atoms join together to form different types of material. The blobs represent individual atoms. The sticks represent the forces that pull the atoms together.

Metals

The atoms in a metal pack together tightly to make a dense, strong material. Electrons find it easy to move from atom to atom through the metal. That's why metal is such a good conductor of electricity.

▷ This picture shows the atomic structure of the metal gold. This metal is extremely ductile—it can be pulled out or hammered into extremely thin sheets without breaking.

Polymers

Polymers include materials such as plastic, rubber, and horn. These materials share an important characteristic. They are all made of long chains of repeating units, called monomers. The monomers themselves are small structures, just a few atoms in size. This picture shows the polymer that makes up rubber. You can see some of its separate monomers, linked together to form the polymer chain. Some polymers are thousands of monomers long.

◁ The joins between these monomers can open and close, almost like the hinges of a door. This is why rubber can bend and stretch without breaking, then return to its original size.

Crystals

The atoms in a crystal join together in a regular, repeating structure. This gives a crystal its regular faces. If light can find a pathway between the atoms in a crystal, all the way through the material, the crystal is transparent. These pictures show the atomic structures of diamond (near right) and graphite (far right). Both these crystals are made from carbon atoms. The arrangement of the atoms in diamond makes it extremely strong. Light can pass easily between the atoms, so diamond is also highly transparent. Graphite is the material that is used to make the lead part of a pencil.

▷ The boxy arrangement of the carbon atoms in diamond make it extremely hard and strong.

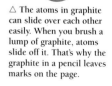

△ The atoms in graphite can slide over each other easily. When you brush a lump of graphite, atoms slide off it. That's why the graphite in a pencil leaves marks on the page.

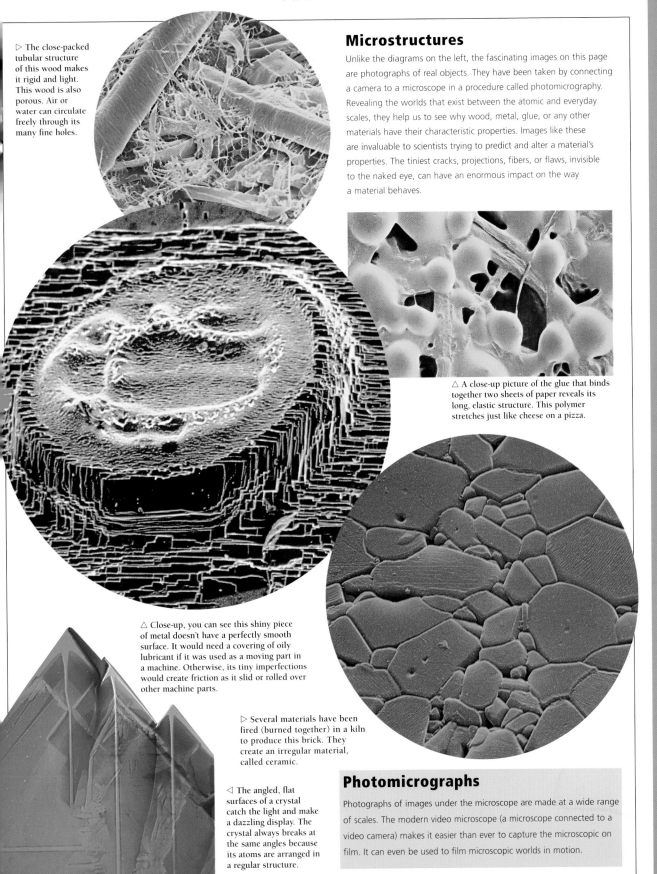

▷ The close-packed tubular structure of this wood makes it rigid and light. This wood is also porous. Air or water can circulate freely through its many fine holes.

Microstructures

Unlike the diagrams on the left, the fascinating images on this page are photographs of real objects. They have been taken by connecting a camera to a microscope in a procedure called photomicrography. Revealing the worlds that exist between the atomic and everyday scales, they help us to see why wood, metal, glue, or any other materials have their characteristic properties. Images like these are invaluable to scientists trying to predict and alter a material's properties. The tiniest cracks, projections, fibers, or flaws, invisible to the naked eye, can have an enormous impact on the way a material behaves.

△ A close-up picture of the glue that binds together two sheets of paper reveals its long, elastic structure. This polymer stretches just like cheese on a pizza.

△ Close-up, you can see this shiny piece of metal doesn't have a perfectly smooth surface. It would need a covering of oily lubricant if it was used as a moving part in a machine. Otherwise, its tiny imperfections would create friction as it slid or rolled over other machine parts.

▷ Several materials have been fired (burned together) in a kiln to produce this brick. They create an irregular material, called ceramic.

◁ The angled, flat surfaces of a crystal catch the light and make a dazzling display. The crystal always breaks at the same angles because its atoms are arranged in a regular structure.

Photomicrographs

Photographs of images under the microscope are made at a wide range of scales. The modern video microscope (a microscope connected to a video camera) makes it easier than ever to capture the microscopic on film. It can even be used to film microscopic worlds in motion.

Powers of ten

Large and small

Every moment of the day, our lives are governed by some of the largest and smallest things that exist in the universe. A human thought, for example, is generated by chemicals that flow from neuron to neuron in the brain. The gap between two neurons, called the synapse, is less than a billionth of a yard wide. On a much larger scale, we experience day and night because the Earth moves around the Sun, which is around 500 billion feet away. As day draws to an end, light from the Sun, a colossal star, no longer reaches the place you are living on Earth. Darkness triggers signals to flow between minuscule neurons in your brain, telling you that it's nighttime. Scientists need to study what goes on at any scale within the universe. To do this, they have developed a measuring system that makes it easy to judge the size of any object— no matter how large or small—in an instant.

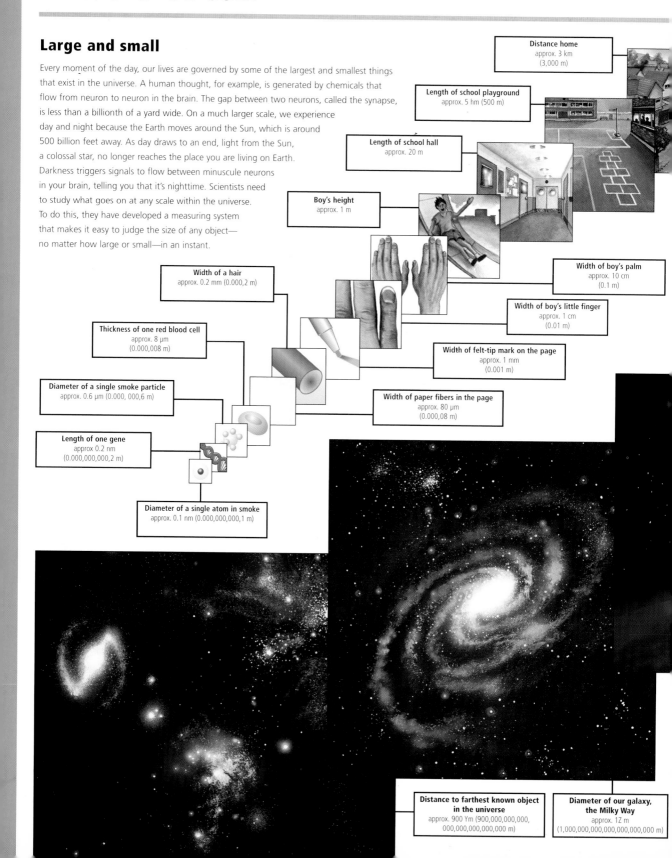

Distance home
approx. 3 km
(3,000 m)

Length of school playground
approx. 5 hm (500 m)

Length of school hall
approx. 20 m

Boy's height
approx. 1 m

Width of boy's palm
approx. 10 cm
(0.1 m)

Width of boy's little finger
approx. 1 cm
(0.01 m)

Width of a hair
approx. 0.2 mm (0.000,2 m)

Width of felt-tip mark on the page
approx. 1 mm
(0.001 m)

Thickness of one red blood cell
approx. 8 μm
(0.000,008 m)

Width of paper fibers in the page
approx. 80 μm
(0.000,08 m)

Diameter of a single smoke particle
approx. 0.6 μm (0.000, 000,6 m)

Length of one gene
approx 0.2 nm
(0.000,000,000,2 m)

Diameter of a single atom in smoke
approx. 0.1 nm (0.000,000,000,1 m)

**Distance to farthest known object
in the universe**
approx. 900 Ym (900,000,000,000,
000,000,000,000,000 m)

**Diameter of our galaxy,
the Milky Way**
approx. 1Z m
(1,000,000,000,000,000,000,000 m)

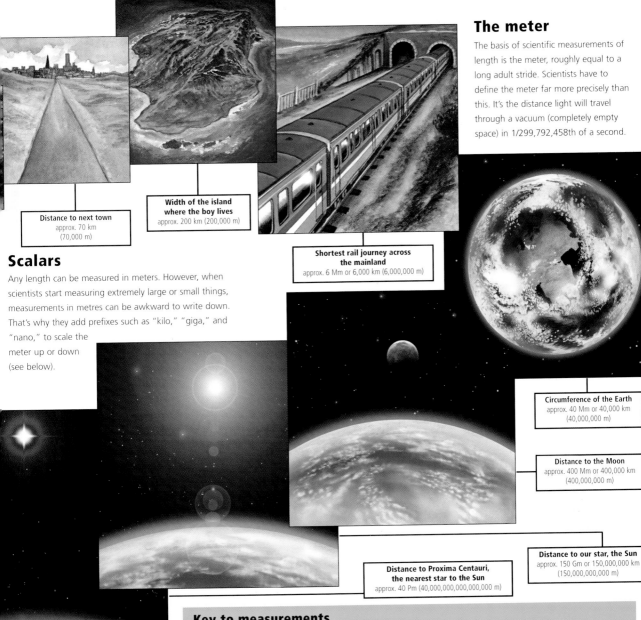

The meter

The basis of scientific measurements of length is the meter, roughly equal to a long adult stride. Scientists have to define the meter far more precisely than this. It's the distance light will travel through a vacuum (completely empty space) in 1/299,792,458th of a second.

Distance to next town
approx. 70 km
(70,000 m)

Width of the island where the boy lives
approx. 200 km (200,000 m)

Scalars

Any length can be measured in meters. However, when scientists start measuring extremely large or small things, measurements in metres can be awkward to write down. That's why they add prefixes such as "kilo," "giga," and "nano," to scale the meter up or down (see below).

Shortest rail journey across the mainland
approx. 6 Mm or 6,000 km (6,000,000 m)

Circumference of the Earth
approx. 40 Mm or 40,000 km
(40,000,000 m)

Distance to the Moon
approx. 400 Mm or 400,000 km
(400,000,000 m)

Distance to our star, the Sun
approx. 150 Gm or 150,000,000 km
(150,000,000,000 m)

Distance to Proxima Centauri, the nearest star to the Sun
approx. 40 Pm (40,000,000,000,000,000 m)

Key to measurements

PREFIX	SYMBOL	SIZE
yotta	Y	a million billion billion (1 Ym = 1,000,000,000,000,000,000,000,000 m)
zetta	Z	a thousand billion billion (1 Zm =1,000,000,000,000,000,000,000 m)
exa	E	a billion billion (1 Em = 1,000,000,000,000,000,000 m)
peta	P	a million billion (1 Pm = 1,000,000,000,000,000 m)
tera	T	a thousand billion (1 Tm = 1,000,000,000,000 m)
giga	G	a billion (1 Gm = 1,000,000,000 m)
mega	M	a million (1 Mm = 1,000,000 m)
kilo	k	a thousand (1 Km = 1,000 m)
hecto	h	a hundred (1 hm = 100 m)
centi	c	a hundredth (1 cm = 0.01 m)
milli	m	a thousandth (1 mm = 0.001 m)
micro	μ	a millionth (1 μm = 0.000,001 m)
nano	n	a billionth (1 nm = 0.000,000,001 m)
pico	p	a thousandth of a billionth (1 pm = 0.000,000,000,001 m)

How scalars work

The box on the right shows you what every prefix means. "Micro," for example, means "a millionth," so a micrometer is a million times smaller than a meter. A shorter way to write micro is μ. Although they both mean the same thing, 5 μm is much easier to write down than 0.000,005 m.

Thinking power

Thinking speed and memory capacity

You are living in a fascinating era, when computers are developing at an astonishing rate. The computer you can buy today is probably twice as fast as the one that was available for the same money just a couple of years ago. Amazingly, since the first automatic calculating machines were introduced around a century ago, the world's most powerful thinking machines have been increasing a thousand times in computing power every 20 years.

Computers have already transformed many areas of life, for example, science, medicine, banking, and entertainment. Anticipating further boosts in computing power, many people are now wondering what these machines will be able to do in the future.

Some of the most interesting predictions were made over ten years ago, by the robotics scientist, Hans Moravec. Working at Carnegie Mellon University, Moravec wrote about the prospect of computers reaching "human equivalence." A computer with human equivalence would be able to store the same amount of data (information) as a human mind and process it at the same speed. In a book called *Mind Children*, Moravec suggested that computers would reach this level within the first half of the 21st century.

To back up his predictions, Moravec produced some graphs of the thinking powers of things that already exist. We've adapted them on these two pages. Moravec stressed that a machine with human equivalence would not necessarily think or act like a human. Its intelligence would largely depend on how it had been wired together and programmed (given instructions to make

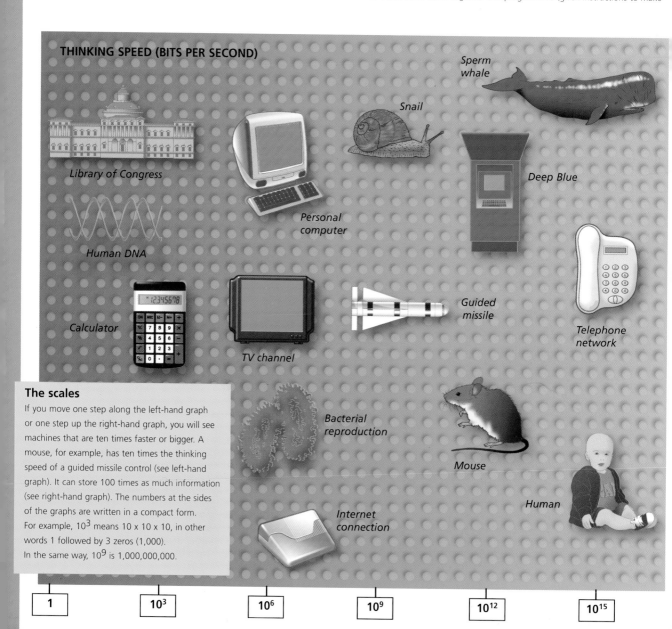

THINKING SPEED (BITS PER SECOND)

Sperm whale

Snail

Library of Congress

Deep Blue

Personal computer

Human DNA

Telephone network

Calculator

Guided missile

TV channel

The scales

If you move one step along the left-hand graph or one step up the right-hand graph, you will see machines that are ten times faster or bigger. A mouse, for example, has ten times the thinking speed of a guided missile control (see left-hand graph). It can store 100 times as much information (see right-hand graph). The numbers at the sides of the graphs are written in a compact form. For example, 10^3 means 10 x 10 x 10, in other words 1 followed by 3 zeros (1,000). In the same way, 10^9 is 1,000,000,000.

Bacterial reproduction

Mouse

Human

Internet connection

| 1 | 10^3 | 10^6 | 10^9 | 10^{12} | 10^{15} |

it work). However, Moravec did believe that computers with humanlike thought would be common by the year 2040. He imagined these machines as another stage of the evolution of life on Earth. Regarding humans as their ancestors, they would be able to think in ways beyond human imagination.

The thinking speed (left-hand) graph compares the speed at which data can be taken from or moved around each system. Data could be words, pictures, videos, sounds, or any other kind of information. Faster systems are farther to the right of the page. The memory size (right-hand) graph compares the amount of data that can be stored by each system. Systems with larger memory sizes are higher up the page. The unit of measurement is a "bit."

A bit is a tiny amount of data, roughly what you'd need to store one letter of a book. You'd need 32 bits just to store the color of a single pixel (dot) of a picture. A full-screen color photograph, or five seconds of CD-quality sound, would need at least a quarter of a million bits of information. The brain doesn't shuffle information around, bit by bit, like a computer. It depends on complex interactions between its neurons, each of which is connected to many others (see page 9). Researchers have studied the capabilities of artificial neural networks. This has helped them to estimate the size of a computer that would have human equivalence. According to Moravec's graph, so far a desktop PC is only as good as a bee!

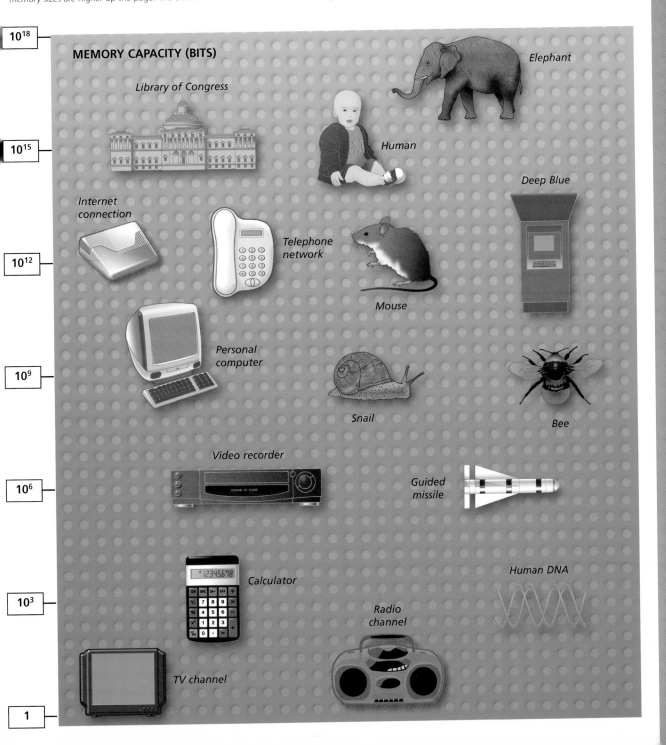

MEMORY CAPACITY (BITS)

- 10^{18}
- 10^{15}
- 10^{12}
- 10^{9}
- 10^{6}
- 10^{3}
- 1

Elephant

Library of Congress

Human

Deep Blue

Internet connection

Telephone network

Mouse

Personal computer

Snail

Bee

Video recorder

Guided missile

Calculator

Human DNA

Radio channel

TV channel

Plants that cure

Useful plants

The millions of plant species in the world contain a treasure-house of medicines. So far, fewer than one in 50 of all plant species has been tested for medicinal properties. Pharmacologists (drug scientists) are keen to continue the search for untested plants that could hold the key to significant new medicines. Unfortunately, they are working against the clock. Pollution, consumption of plant materials, and changes in land use have put many of the world's plant species in danger. If humans carry on destroying the world's biodiversity at the current rate, around 20 percent of the world's species will have disappeared by the year 2020. One in four of the drugs that may be prescribed by a doctor is based on chemicals found in plants. Some are extracted from plants themselves. Others are made in a laboratory to mimic plant-based chemicals. Here are just ten of the invaluable plant-based drugs that are around today.

Cinchona

Used for countless centuries by the native peoples of China and South America, the bark of the cinchona tree contains quinine, a powerful antidote to malaria. Europeans have known about cinchona from the time they first colonized the Americas, around 400 years ago. Malaria is still the biggest single killer on the planet. This disease, which is carried by mosquitoes, kills around four people every minute. In the early part of this century, a shortage of cinchona trees led scientists to search for a synthetic version of quinine. They made this from coal tar. Unfortunately, synthetic antimalarial drugs have been used so heavily around the world that the disease has grown resistant to them (see pages 18–19). Scientists are now studying natural quinine again, to try to understand the properties that make it so good at fighting malaria.

Coca

The drugs Novocaine and Lidocaine are used to relieve pain in dentistry and surgery. These anesthetics, which are both made in the laboratory, are safer versions of cocaine, the herbal drug on which they are both based. Cocaine itself comes from the leaves of the coca plant, which grows widely in South America. Although we most often think of cocaine as a dangerous, habit-forming drug, it paved the way for some of our most important painkillers.

Curare

An arrow poison, used by hunters in the Amazon rainforests, forms the basis of the surgical drug curare. The most important active ingredient in curare comes from the bark or vines of certain plants that grow in South America. Originally used to paralyze animals, curare works in a very strange way. It stops nerve pulses from traveling to and from most of the muscles in the body, but does not disrupt the beating of the heart. Safe drugs, based on curare, are used to keep an anesthetized person on the operating table completely relaxed and still.

Digitalis

A very important heart drug comes from a flower called the foxglove. The drug itself, called digitalis, regulates heart rate and helps the body to remove excess fluid. Before the effectiveness of the foxglove was recognized in the 18th century, many people with heart problems used to suffer from a terrible disease called dropsy. With a weakened heart, fluid would collect within their body, puffing it out into a grotesque shape and making them very weak.

Ergotamine

A fungus that grows on rye, wheat, or barley has given us drugs that can ease migraine and stop too much blood loss during difficult childbirth. Called ergot, this fungus is highly poisonous when eaten raw. It causes hallucinations, gangrene (rotting limbs), and eventual death. However, the active ingredients extracted from ergot make powerful, safe drugs. These work partly by narrowing the vessels (tubes) that carry blood around the body.

Mayapple

We know that humans have been using plants to treat cancers for at least 3,500 years, and today pharmacists continue their search for new cancer therapies. Researchers are hoping that extracts from plant materials will form the basis for new, synthetic drugs. The small, white-flowering plant mayapple is just one of the plants they are studying. A drug, called etopside, extracted from this plant, stops the DNA in cells from copying itself. In this way, it halts the production of cancerous and healthy cells.

Pacific yew

Until recently, a promising new anticancer drug that can save many lives required the destruction of a rare tree. Called Taxol, the drug slows down the growth rate of some types of tumor. The active ingredients in Taxol used to come only from the bark of the Pacific yew tree, which is an endangered species (see pages 34–5). Around four trees need to be destroyed to make enough Taxol for just one patient. Researchers have been adapting the chemicals found in other, more common yew trees, and even filbert shells, to find alternative sources of Taxol.

Potato

The humble potato may one day be the carrier for life-saving edible vaccines. About 3 million children a year die from diarrhea caused by E. coli, most of them in the poorer, developing countries where there are often poor refrigeration facilities for conventional vaccines. Potato vaccines could offer a lifeline to these children. In a trial, scientists took out some genes from potatoes and replaced them with genes for an E. coli vaccine. When slices of this potato were given to children in danger, they were protected from E. coli. These early tests suggest that edible vaccines could have a future. They could be delivered around the world as easily as dried fruit.

Rice

A rice that has been genetically modified to carry vitamin A could save the lives of millions of people a year. However, until this genetically modified (GM) rice passes tough safety tests, it can't be sold as a food crop. The company that developed the rice realized that millions of people die each year because they are short of vitamin A—the vitamin that we commonly pick up from red or orange food such as carrots. Vitamin A gives you resistance to many diseases. Scientists decided to take the genes that make vitamin A in daffodils and splice them into the DNA of ordinary rice. People who eat the GM rice that these researchers have produced will pick up the life-saving vitamin A as part of their ordinary diet.

Yam

A staple food for millions around the world, yam is also an abundant source of medicines. This vegetable contains a chemical called diosgenin that can be used to make various useful chemicals for the body. In the laboratory, yams can also be used to make the hormone progesterone. Scientists need a supply of this hormone in order to study how it influences human health. Progesterone is helpful for older women, for example, because it helps their bones remain dense and strong.

Genetics breakthroughs

DATE	EVENT

c. 570 B.C. The Greek philosopher ..Anaximander writes that all life comes from the sea and that animals formed different characteristics because they adapted to their new surroundings. He also says that humans descended from other species.

1655 A.D. Robert Hooke, England, becomes the first person to see cells under a microscope.

1749 Carolus Linnaeus, from Sweden, develops a systematic way to name, rank, and classify (sort) all living things. He divides them into distinct species (for example, cats, birds, and frogs) which are grouped into genera, families of species with similar characteristics. The work of Linnaeus paves the way for later theories of evolution. His naming methods are still used today.

c..1800 Comte de Bouffon, France, suggests that similar animals are descended from common ancestors. His work heavily influences the naturalist Charles Darwin.

1824 René Dutrochet, France, discovers that the cell is the basic building block in the structure of all living things.

1838 German botanist Matthias Schleiden finds that all plants are made of cells.

1839 Theodor Schwann, Germany, states that all living things are composed of cells. He shows the egg is a single cell and discovers that all animal cells have a nucleus.

1857 Gregor Mendel, born in Czechoslovakia, discovers how traits are passed down from one generation of a living thing to another. His work, based on experiments with pea plants, is published in 1865.

1859 British naturalist Charles Darwin publishes *On the Origin of Species by Means of Natural Selection*, explaining his theory of evolution. By agreement, it was published at exactly the same time as the writings of another British naturalist, Alfred Russell Wallace, who had very similar theories.

1869 British scientist Francis Galton, cousin of Charles Darwin, publishes *Hereditary Genius*. In this book he suggests, wrongly, that intelligence is inherited in a simple manner. His work lays the foundations for eugenics, a distasteful political idea loosely based on genetics. Eugenicists argue that only people with the right traits for the future of the human race should be allowed to have children.

1882 After staining cells with dye, the German biologist Walther Flemming discovers tiny rods in their nuclei. He calls them chromosomes.

1887 Edouard van Beneden, Belgian zoologist, finds that an animal has the same number of chromosomes in every cell of its body, except its sex cells (sperm or egg) which have half the usual number. This discovery was invaluable to later scientists studying inheritance. Van Beneden also discovers that the number of chromosomes varies from animal to animal.

1903 British doctor Archibald Garrod shows some diseases are caused by inherited genes, paving the way for genetic testing and therapies.

1908 Experimenting on the fruit fly, Thomas Hunt Morgan, U.S., shows for the first time that tiny units within chromosomes pass down traits from parents to offspring. These units are now called genes.

1944 The American doctor Oswald Theodore Avery confirms that our chromosomes are made from a long molecule called DNA. Genes are small excerpts of this DNA molecule. Avery shows that DNA is responsible for a living thing's inherited traits.

c.1948 American scientist Edwin Chargraff notices that every species has a different type of DNA. He also discovers how simpler molecules combine to make DNA.

Tree seed-eating finch

Tree insect-eating finch

View through Hooke's microscope

Hooke's microscope

It was during a trip around the world on HMS *Beagle* that Charles Darwin gathered evidence for his theory of evolution. This theory developed as he documented the variations between animals on his trip. On the Galapagos Islands in the Pacific Ocean, he noted that closely related species of finch had different shaped beaks. The beak shapes have evolved depending on the finches' food supply.

Ground seed-eating finch

Seed-eater

Robert Hooke was studying cork through a new microscope when he saw it was made of thousands of small units. He was the first to call these units "cells."

Although he was a brilliant genetics pioneer, Gregor Mendel's experimental results are treated with scepticism. It's likely he fudged them to make them fit in with his theories.

Bud- and leaf-eating finch

1952 James Dewey Watson and Francis Crick, both working in Britain, discover that the atoms that form the DNA molecule are arranged in a double helix shape (two interweaving spirals).

1957 Arthur Kornberg, U.S., extracts DNA from the *E. coli* bacteria—the first time that DNA molecules have been extracted.

c.1966 Various scientists discover the genetic code—the way in which DNA acts as an instruction book, telling a living thing how to grow and work.

1969 Scientists at Harvard Medical School isolate a single gene.

1970s Researchers in Britain clone tadpoles from eggs. The clones do not fully mature.

1973 Herbert Boyer, U.S., splices DNA from one species into another, to make a living thing called a chimera, for the first time. His work uses techniques pioneered by fellow American, Paul Berg.

1982 Human insulin, the first genetically engineered drug, is approved for sale.

1984 Harvard research scientists receive a U.S. patent for the oncomouse. This is a breed of mouse that has been genetically engineered to be more likely to develop cancers. Used in cancer research, the oncomouse is the first patented mammal.

1985 Alec Jeffreys and his colleagues in Britain invent the DNA fingerprint, an image that allows identification of someone's genetic code. The DNA fingerprint is first used for disputes over parentage of babies, but is soon adapted for crime detection.

1986 Sheep and cattle are cloned from embryos in the U.S. and Britain.

A genetically engineered tobacco plant is grown in test plantations. This is the first time a GM (genetically modified) crop is tested outside the laboratory.

1988 The Human Genome Project, a worldwide project to map the entire genetic code in human DNA, begins.

1989 While studying the disease sickle cell anemia, Kary Mullis invents PCR, a way to duplicate a small fragment of DNA so it can be tested more easily. PCR becomes an invaluable tool in forensic science and paleontology.

1990 The first gene therapies are attempted. Results are mixed.

The first GM food ingredient goes on the market. It's chymosin, a chemical to replace the rennet used in cheesemaking. Many vegetarians choose not to eat rennet because it comes from slaughtered cattle.

1993 A company is allowed to feed genetically engineered materials to cattle to increase their milk production. Anxiety about the safety of genetically modified food grows among the public.

1994 The FlavrSavr tomato goes on the market, initially in the U.S. The first GM whole food, this tomato has been genetically engineered to have a longer shelf life.

1995 A baboon is given the heart of a genetically altered pig, in the world's first transgenic xenotransplant (transplant between two different species). The baboon only lives for a few hours.

1997 The first mammal, a sheep called Dolly, is cloned from an ordinary adult cell by researchers in Britain. A few days later, researchers in the U.S. claim to have produced the first primate clones: two rhesus monkeys.

1997 The researchers who produced Dolly announce the arrival of Polly, a cloned transgenic sheep. Some of her genetic material has been replaced with human DNA. In the future, a herd of sheep like Polly could produce chemicals in their milk for use in human medicines.

1998 A company announces it will have finished decoding the entire human genome— completing the Human Genome Project—by 2001.

1999 Researchers notice signs of Dolly's premature aging. As she was cloned from an adult cell, her telomeres (see page 57) have frayed very early in her life span.

2000 The Icelandic people give a private company the right to survey their genetic code.

Watson and Crick developed their double helix theory by modeling DNA with cardboard and wire. Their work owed a great debt to earlier breakthrough research by Maurice Wilkins and Rosalind Franklin.

Many geneticists use a type of fruit fly, called *Drosophila*, in their experiments. *Drosophila* is popular because it is easy to keep, it breeds very quickly, and it only has four pairs of chromosomes.

Millions of diabetics around the world depend on regular doses of the drug insulin. Before it could be grown from genetically engineered bacteria, this life-saving drug was extracted from dead sheep and pigs.

Pigs with human genes are sparking the latest genetics controversy. They could offer organs for human transplant. But there is concern that this could spread diseases from pigs to humans.

Space exploration

Future missions

Astronauts first stepped on the Moon more than 30 years ago. Their mission, on the *Apollo 11* spacecraft, was the first to take people to a destination outside Earth. A huge team of space scientists and engineers enabled the *Apollo* crew to reach the Moon. And they didn't stop dreaming about space exploration when the Moon landings were over. Along with their successors, they have a whole list of missions that they would like to attempt in the future. On these pages we look at a few of the items on their list.

△ International Space Station
Status: under assembly in
space, ready for crew in 2004.

▽ Stardust probe
Status: launched in 1999.

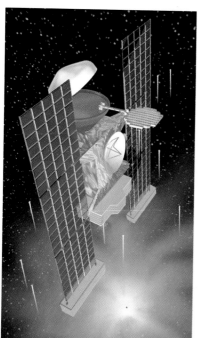

International Space Station

The International Space Station (ISS) is already being assembled in space. Sixteen countries are helping to construct this floating laboratory, which should be ready for its entire crew of scientists in 2004. The experiments carried out on the ISS may help scientists to develop new materials and medicines. They may also enable scientists to find better ways to support astronauts during long-term space missions.

Space weather forecasting

Launched in December 1995, a spacecraft that is now about 1,000,000 miles from the Earth is keeping watch on the Sun. Called SOHO, it monitors ripples on the surface of the Sun around 93 million miles away. Back on Earth, scientists study these ripples to guess what's happening on the other side of the Sun. They use this information to predict solar storms. A satellite called IMAGE, launched in 2000, will study the effect of solar storms back on Earth. It will see how they disrupt the Earth's delicate magnetic field. Together, SOHO and IMAGE will improve space weather forecasting in the future.

Stardust probe

If all goes according to plan, this space probe will be the first ever to brush past a comet. Nanotechnologists have put a tiny chip inside Stardust, packed with the names of 130,000 people who want to send a message into space. Launched in 1999, the Stardust probe will take five years to reach the comet Wild-2. In that time, the probe will have traveled over 1.85 billion miles to its meeting place, sweeping twice around the Sun. On its journey, it will collect some of the tiny specks of stardust that sweep through the solar system. After its close encounter with Wild-2, Stardust will return to Earth where its samples can be studied.

Icebreaker

Still on the drawing board, Icebreaker will help us to work out the long-term prospects for a human colony on the Moon. This spacecraft will go to the Moon's poles, searching for frozen water. Icebreaker follows on from the work of an earlier probe, Lunar Prospector. This caused a worldwide sensation when it found traces of hydrogen on the Moon, possibly from frozen water. If there is a natural reservoir of water on the Moon, it will be much easier to set up a lunar colony. The water can be used to make breathable oxygen, as well as for a drinking supply. Hydrogen in the water could be used as rocket fuel for further missions or to bring a crew home.

Muses-C

Like Stardust, Muses-C is a small probe, designed to collect samples and bring them back to Earth. A partnership between scientists in the U.S. and Japan, Muses-C is destined to meet an asteroid. The solar system is full of asteroids, fragments of rock that orbit the Sun. Most are the debris left behind when the planets and moons were forming. A closer look at an asteroid may help us to work out the early history of the solar system. Muses-C, due for launch in 2002, will meet an asteroid codenamed 1989ML.

Lunar return

If the Icebreaker project (see opposite) finds water, it may encourage governments to fund a mission back to the Moon. No human has stepped on the Moon since the *Apollo 17* astronaut Gene Cernan took his final step off the lunar surface on December 14, 1972. A small human colony established on the Moon could carry out many scientific experiments. Scientists have been imagining these for many years. The Moon has been called a geologist's paradise. It's the perfect place to study how craters, volcanoes, the Moon, and the Earth were formed. Unlike Earth, the Moon has no atmosphere and is not troubled by earthquakes. This also makes it the ideal location for highly sensitive telescopes that could picture the universe in even finer detail than the Hubble Space Telescope (see page 39). As they experiment on the Moon, the inhabitants of a lunar colony may also develop the skills and technology needed to build other space settlements farther afield.

▽This picture shows Mars in the early stages of terraforming. The crew working on the planet are still relying on breathing equipment. As the effects of terraforming can't be fully predicted, many people question whether we should tamper with the climate of Mars at all.

Reaching Mars

We already know how to send a crew to Mars, but plans for such a trip have been outrageously expensive. To keep within its budget, the American space agency NASA has sent robots to the planet instead. While these rovers explored the surface of Mars at the end of the 1990s, people watched them from Earth. These robot missions were safer as well as cheaper than any mission with a crew. NASA is planning more robot missions to Mars, right up to the year 2009. Among other tasks, these robots could identify safe landing sites for later, crewed ships. A trip to Mars would take six months each way—a very long time to spend in space. Experiments planned on the International Space Station will help scientists to plan such a trip.

Terraforming

Humans would not find Mars a very welcoming planet. As far as we can tell, it has no water and no atmosphere to sustain human life. A Martian colony would have to bring its own water, food, and air supply. Otherwise, it would need to make these from the resources available on the planet. One possible solution would be to "terraform" the planet to make it more like home. The first step would be to heat the planet slightly, turning the planet's supply of frozen carbon dioxide into gas. The carbon dioxide would trap heat from the Sun, warming the planet further. If any single-celled animals were introduced to Mars, they would use this carbon dioxide to make oxygen. They would create an atmosphere in which humans and plants could survive. However, terraforming would be a hugely risky operation. It's difficult to predict what would happen if any part of the process went wrong—for example, if the planet became too warm for plants to thrive.

△ Icebreaker
Status: due for possible launch about 2003.

△ Lunar return
Status: still under discussion, scientifically possible now.

◁ Muses-C
Status: due for launch in 2002.

△Terraforming Mars
Status: possible only in long-term future, many technical obstacles and uncertainties still to be overcome.

▽ Clone This sheep, codenamed, Dolly, caused a worldwide sensation when she was born in 1997. Contrary to many newspaper reports, Dolly wasn't the first-ever clone. She was the first mammal ever to be cloned, using DNA from an ordinary adult cell.

▽ Black Hole. Many black holes can only be detected by watching objects nearby being pulled toward them. A few black holes are easier to spot because they throw out telltale X-rays. These X-rays come from matter that is swirling around the black hole, like water around a plughole.

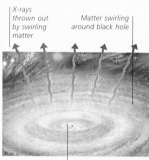

X-rays thrown out by swirling matter

Matter swirling around black hole

black hole

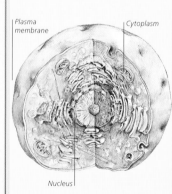

Plasma membrane

Cytoplasm

Nucleus

△ Cell. Scientists first began to study cells only 350 years ago. Today, they are looking closely at the material that lies within the cell's nucleus (center). In particular, they are starting to unravel the purpose of DNA, the molecule that carries a living thing's genetic code. This influences how any living thing grows, develops, and acts.

Glossary

absolute zero A temperature of around –459° F. Nothing in the universe can get colder than this.

alloy A mixture of materials, completely or partly metal. Brass is an alloy, as is the superconductor vanadium-silicon.

annihilation In particle physics, this is what happens when matter and antimatter collide. They completely destroy each other, disappearing in a burst of pure energy.

antimatter A substance made of particles that have opposite characteristics (for example, opposite charge or opposite magnetic properties). Some stars, even entire galaxies, could be made of antimatter.

antibiotics Drugs that can attack and kill bacteria. They are used to combat infections in living things.

artificial intelligence (AI) A branch of science that is trying to develop machines that can sense their surroundings and make decisions, just like humans. Machines with limited forms of artificial intelligence are already in use.

atom The minuscule building block of all substances in the universe. An atom is about a nanometer in diameter. It is made up of protons, neutrons, and electrons.

bacteria Tiny living things, usually made of a single cell. They are also called germs. Unwanted bacteria can cause infections in humans and other living things.

bacteriophage A virus that is able to destroy a certain type of bacteria by getting inside their cells and multiplying. Bacteriophages are being studied as possible alternatives to antibiotics.

Big Bang The explosive event that happened around 15 billion years ago, at the moment the universe began.

Big Crunch After billions of years expanding, the universe could deflate again, eventually coming together in the Big Crunch, a reverse of the Big Bang.

billion A thousand million (1,000,000,000).

biodiversity The amount of variety that exists among plants, animals and other living things that share the planet.

biomass Wood, dung, and other material from plants and animals that can be burned for fuel.

Black hole An extremely dense collapsed star or other object that pulls everything nearby toward it. Not even light can travel fast enough to escape a black hole.

cell The basic unit of living things and their tissues. A human body is built out of billions of cells.

Chaos theory A branch of mathematics that searches for patterns and predicts what will happen in seemingly random situations. Possible uses include forecasting the weather and timing irregular heartbeats.

chimera A creature made by mixing the cells from two different living species. A shoat, for example, is made by mixing together the cells of a sheep and a goat.

chromosome A collection of thousands of genes inside the nucleus of a living cell. Most humans have 46 chromosomes. These contain all the genes that make up their DNA.

clone A living thing, produced artificially, that is genetically identical to one of its parents. A clone is produced in the laboratory by grafting a parent's DNA into an egg cell.

cryogenics A branch of science and engineering that studies the way things behave at very cold temperatures.

dark matter Material, thought to make up a large part of the universe, that so far lies undetected.

DNA (Deoxyribonucleic acid) The chemical in the nucleus of every cell of a living thing that carries its unique genetic code.

DNA fingerprint An image, quite like a bar code, that shows the genetic pattern of part of someone's DNA. Unless you are an identical twin, your DNA fingerprint is unique.

electronic paper A thin sheet, still under development, that can be written on using a pen but erased electronically. Electronic paper can also be loaded with pictures or images from a computer.

epidemiology A branch of medicine that studies patterns of disease. Epidemiologists look for lifestyle patterns that are connected with diseases. For example, they confirmed the link between smoking and lung cancer.

evolution The changes that happen to plants and animals over thousands of generations. The living things that are best suited to their surroundings are the ones most likely to survive and produce offspring (called natural selection). They pass their traits on to their offspring. This is the process of evolution.

fractal A complex, seemingly random-looking pattern, made by repeating a simple shape in a particular, mathematical way. Fractals are used to draw clouds, mountains, and other natural backgrounds in some computer games.

fusion reactor A machine that can fuse the nuclei of atoms together, making larger nuclei and releasing intense bursts of energy. A practical fusion reactor could become a source of clean, safe power.

gene A fragment of the DNA molecule that does a particular job. A gene can influence the look of a living thing, how it works, how it behaves, or even how it develops. All the genes in a living thing arrange themselves into a few dozen rod-shaped units called chromosomes.

genetics The branch of science that studies genes, how they are inherited, and how they influence living things. Genetics can help to explain the way we inherit traits from our parents.

geothermal energy Energy that is taken from underground steam or produced by passing water over hot, underground rocks.

germline therapy A medical treatment that involves changing genes in all of a person's cells, including ones they will pass on to any future children.

gluon The particle thought to make the force that keeps quarks together.

Great Annihilator The black hole at the center of the Milky Way.

Hubble A huge optical telescope that has been orbiting Earth since 1990. As its view isn't obscured by the Earth's atmosphere, Hubble can see to the farthest reaches of the universe.

human-computer interface The part of a computer system that we can see, feel, hear, or touch. Examples include a screen, keyboard, and dataglove.

Human Genome Project The giant worldwide project to work out the pattern of genes that make up human DNA. The project was finished in 2000.

International Space Station A large space station that will hold people in orbit around the Earth. Due for completion in 2004, it will be used to find out more about living, working, and growing crops in space.

IVF Bringing sperm and an egg together, in the laboratory, to help them to make new life. IVF, which stands for "in vitro fertilization," is used to help people who are having trouble producing children.

keystone species A plant or animal on which many other living things in the area rely, directly or indirectly, for their survival.

lightsail A spacecraft that is powered by photons from the Sun. The spacecraft moves forward when photons hit its giant, lightweight sail.

matter The name for any substance in the universe—from water to a cosmic dust cloud. Technically, matter is anything that has a mass.

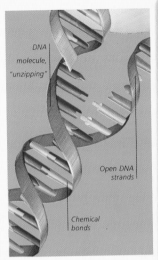

△ DNA. The double-helix structure of DNA (see page 12) enables it to "unzip," so it can copy itself from CELL to cell. The two halves of an unzipped DNA molecule attract new chemicals. These enable it to build two entirely new copies of itself.

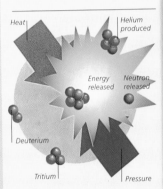

△ Fusion. A fusion reactor, which releases energy by bringing light atoms together, produces power in the same way as the Sun.

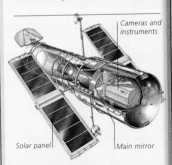

△ Hubble space telescope. Hubble was designed for easy maintenance in space. Using models of Hubble on Earth, astronauts practiced how to spacewalk around Hubble to carry out repairs.

▽ Nebula The dust within a nebula can cluster together to form new stars and planets. The nebula itself could be the debris left behind by a star that died in a colossal explosion, called a supernova. A supernova can light up a huge patch of the night sky.

The dust in the Eagle nebula could eventually form new stars and plane

1 A cluster of bright new stars emerges from a cloud of gas and dust.

2 Hot gas from the stars triggers the formation of more stars in the cloud.

3 A second cluster of stars emerges and triggers more star formation.

▽ Multiverse. While the idea of many branching universes fits some mathematical theories, there's no firm physical evidence that a multiverse exists. Even so, the theory has excited a few computer scientists. They would like to hide secret information by putting it in another universe!

microgravity The tiny gravitational forces that are produced between small objects, for example an astronaut and a spaceship, pulling them together.

million A thousand thousands (1,000,000).

multiverse A collection of two or more connected universes. A few physicists have suggested that our own universe could be part of a giant multiverse.

nanometer A billionth of a meter, or a millionth of a millimeter. This is roughly the diameter of a typical atom.

nanotechnology A branch of engineering that tries to make working machines that are nanometers in size, in other words the size of just a few atoms. Some nanotechnologists try to design and build new materials and working machines atom by atom.

nebula A cloud of dust in space. Stars are formed when the dust in a nebula clusters together.

neural network A set of computer parts that are joined together like neurones (nerve cells). Neural networks can be used to mimic parts of the brain and research how they work.

nucleus The core of a cell or atom.

paleontology A branch of science that studies fossils and other remains to learn about ancient or extinct living things. Many paleontologists research our humanlike ancestors.

particle accelerator A machine that accelerates particles close to the speed of light, then smashes them together. Scientists study the debris from particle accelerator collisions to investigate the building blocks of the universe.

photon The tiny, lightweight particles that make up light.

plasma A gas that is so hot, its electrons have "boiled" away, leaving it electrically charged.

plasma drive A spacecraft that contains a ball of plasma. It funnels particles from the solar wind close to this The solar wind and plasma repel each other, pushing the spacecraft along.

prototype A trial version of a product, such as a car. It is tested and changed as necessary before the real product is manufactured.

quantum telepathy The curious communication that exists between two particles that have been combined in a special way, called entanglement. When you change one particle, its entangled partner will change, too, even if it is in a distant galaxy.

quark The particle that is thought to make up protons and neutrons. Theories suggest that three quarks make up each of these particles. Although scientists have plenty of evidence that quarks exist, they have not been able to capture one.

red giant The appearance of a star during one of its stages of death. When the star runs out of fuel, it disappears as a huge red puff of gas.

remote sensing the process of scanning Earth from space with an instrument such as a camera.

SETI A scientific project to look for telltale signs of alien life. Its full name is "The Search for Extraterrestrial Intelligence."

shape memory alloy (SMA) An alloy that remembers its original shape. When you buckle or bend a shape memory alloy, you can usually easily return it to its original shape, for example, by gently warming it.

singularity Something that is created when a huge amount of matter is packed into a single point in space. The whole universe was packed into a singularity that exploded to form space, matter, and time at the moment of the Big Bang, around 15 billion years ago.

smart material A material that can sense and react to its surroundings. An example would be a piece of concrete, used to make a bridge, that changes color when it is overloaded.

solar cell A material that can turn sunlight into electricity.

solar wind The stream of particles that rip from the Sun and travel through our solar system. The strength of the solar wind varies and is greatest after a solar flare.

somatic therapy A medical treatment that involves changing the genes in some of a person's cells. Somatic therapy never changes a person's reproductive cells so its benefits are not passed down to any future children.

space-time The term scientists use to describe space and time, which they consider to be two types of the same thing.

subatomic particle One of the particles that makes up an atom. Electrons, protons, and neutrons are subatomic particles. Protons and neutrons, in turn, are made of even smaller particles, called quarks. At present, scientists don't think that electrons are made up of smaller particles.

supercomputer An extremely powerful fast computer, that is used to carry out many calculations at once, for example to forecast the weather.

superconductor A material that offers no resistance to the flow of electricity. At the present, scientists only know how to make superconductors that work at very low temperatures – cooler than −150° F.

supernova The explosion of a dying, giant star. For a few days, a supernova can be around 100 billion times brighter than our Sun as it scatters debris into surrounding space.

sustainability The extent to which an activity uses Earth's resources without endangering their future supply. Sustainable fishing, for example, would take mature fish out of the water, but leave plenty of young fish behind.

thought experiment An imaginary experiment, used to demonstrate or explain an unusual idea. The Chinese Room is an example.

teleporter Still only science fiction, this is a machine that can transport anything, including people, from one place to another in an instant.

telesurgery A medical operation controlled by a surgeon who is not in the same room as the patient. In theory, a telesurgeon could operate on a patient in a different city. Early experiments in telesurgery use tools controlled by remote connected computers.

telomere The end of a chromosome. Telomeres suffer wear and tear as a living thing ages. As this wear and tear stops the chromosomes from working properly, it could be a cause of aging and eventual death.

tissue factory A laboratory that can grow real human tissue to order, for instance skin, bone, liver, and brain cells. Most tissue factories are still only experimental.

trait A characteristic of a living thing. Some traits, such as eye color, are inherited. Scientists are still debating whether other traits are inherited, too.

transgenic Containing genes from a different species. Scientists are currently rearing transgenic pigs, for example, that have been given human genes. They hope these pigs will grow organs that are suitable for life-saving transplants.

Turing Test A test for computer intelligence, proposed by the computer pioneer Alan Turing. A computer passes the test if its replies to questions cannot be distinguished from human replies.

Twin Paradox A puzzle that results from the properties of space and time. It concerns twin boys, one of whom travels in a high-speed spaceship. When they meet up again, he has aged far less than his brother who stayed on Earth.

wormhole A theoretical passageway through space-time or even from one universe to the other. Wormholes are made by interconnecting black holes.

xenotransplant An organ transplanted from one species to another, for example, from a pig to a human.

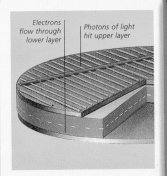

Electrons flow through lower layer

Photons of light hit upper layer

△ Solar cell. When a ray of sunlight shines on a solar cell, photons in the light bump into atoms in the top layer of the cell. They give the atoms enough energy to throw out electrons. These electrons flow into the layer below, making an electric current.

▷ Subatomic particles. Scientists are still figuring out how an atom stays together. In particular, they're trying to discover why protons and neutrons in the atomic nucleus stay clustered together so tightly. They think every proton and neutron is made of three, even smaller particles, called quarks.

Nucleus

3 quarks combine to make a proton or neutron

A mysterious, forcelike quality binds the quarks together so they can make protons and neutrons. It also enables the protons and neutrons to cluster together in the atomic nucleus.

▽ Telomeres. The DNA used to make Dolly the sheep (see page 90) came from another adult ewe. This second-hand DNA had telomeres that were already frayed. Scientists are concerned that these will make Dolly age prematurely.

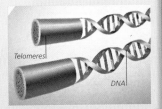

Telomeres

DNA

Index

Acknowledgments

Photographic credits

t = top; b = bottom; c = center; r = right; l = left

9t Carlos Munoz – Yague/Eurelios/Science Photo Library, 9b Klaus Guldbrandsen/Science Photo Library, 9c Adrian Weinbrecht; 10l Peter Menzel/Science Photo Library, 10r James King – Holmes/Science Photo Library, 10–11 Donna Coveney/MIT; 12 Carlos Munoz – Yague/Eurelios/Science Photo Library; 13t Volker Steger/Science Photo Library, 13c James King – Holmes/Science Photo Library, 13b Peter J Oxford/Planet Earth Pictures; 14t Dr John Brackenburg/Science Photo Library, 14b & 15 Geoff Tompkinson/Science Photo Library; 16t Custom Medical Stock Photo/Science Photo Library, 16b SIU/Science Photo Library; 17t Prasad Shastri/MIT, 17b TEK Image/Science Photo Library, 17c The Image Bank; 18c CNRI/Science Photo Library, 18b Associated Press, 18–19 Public Health Laboratory Service; 19t Hulton Getty, 19c The Image Bank, 19b Adrian Weinbrecht; 20t & b, 21t CERN, 21c CERN/Science Photo Library; 22t Mertin Bond/Science Photo Library, 22l JET Laboratory, 22r Honda; 23t Corbis, 23b Roger de la Harpe/Planet Earth Pictures; 24l Biophoto Associates/Science Photo Library, 24c Cornell University, 24–25 Eye of Science/Science Photo Library; 25c Sam Ogden/Science Photo Library, 25b Volker Steger/Saudia National Laboratory/Science Photo Library; 26t John Mead/Science Photo Library, 26b Charlie Waite/Tony Stone, 26–27 Adrian Weinbrecht; 27t Sinclair Stammers/Science Photo Library; 28t, l & r NASA/Science Photo Library, 28b Frank Whitney/The Image Bank; 29b Peter Menzel/Science Photo Library; 30l Tony Stone, 30r BSIP Laurent/Science Photo Library; 31b Activision, 31c William M Smithey/Planet Earth Pictures; 32t Terje Rakke/The Image Bank, 32c Conor Caffrey/Science Photo Library; 33t Adrian Weinbrecht, 33r K.H. Kjeldsen/Science Photo Library, 33c NASA/Science Photo Library 33b D.A. Peel/Science Photo Library; 34 J Eastcott – Y Momatiuk/Planet Earth Pictures; 35t Gary Bell, Matt Richmond/Planet Earth Pictures, 35b Royal Botanic Gardens, Kew; 36–37 NASA; 38t Rosenfeld Images Ltd/Science Photo Library, 38b Paramount TV; 39 NASA; 40t Brian Bailey/Tony Stone, 40b Matthew McVay/Tony Stone, 40–41 Dr Tony Brain/Science Photo Library; 41t Dr Yorgos Nikas/Science Photo Library, 41b Daudier/Sanofi/Jerrican/Science Photo Library; 42t Laura Wickenden, 42b Jeff Christensen/Reuters/Popperfoto; 43 Charles Thatcher/Tony Stone; 45 Roslin Institute; 47t & cr NASA/Science Photo Library, 47c Adastra/Telegraph Colour Library, 47b NASA; 48r Natural History Museum Picture Library; 49tl Hulton Getty, 49tr Bernard Regent/Hutchison Library; 50t A.T. Willett/The Image Bank, 50c Novosti; 51 NASA; 52 David Parker/Science Photo Library; 53t W Bokelberg/The Image Bank, 53b Adam G Sylvester/Science Photo Library; 54t David Weintraub/Science Photo Library, 54c Vincent Realmuto/JPL/Caltech/Science Photo Library, 54b B Murton/Southampton Oceanography Centre/Science Photo Library; 55t Bernhard Edmaier/Science Photo Library, 55c Dr Robert Spicer/Science Photo Library; 56–57 London Archaeology Service; 58tl The Image Bank, 58c Hank Morgan/Science Photo Library, 58b GJLP/Science Photo Library, 58–59 Will & Denny McIntyre/Science Photo Library; 59br David Parker/IMI/University of Birmingham High TC Consortium/Science Photo Library, 59b inset Pacific Press Service/Science Photo Library; 60tl Steve Niedorf/The Image Bank, 60–61; 61t & b Hank Morgan/Science Photo Library, 61 inset NASA/Science Photo Library; 62–63, 64 Michael Roberts/Arrows, 67t Microfield Scientific Ltd/Science Photo Library, 67cl & r Manfred Kage/Science Photo Library, 67bl Eye of Science/Science Photo Library; 72–73 Digitalvision; 75r Roslin Institute; 76–77 NASA.

Dividers: Storyfile: Alfred Pasieka/Science Photo Library, Jobfile: Michael Roberts; Overview, In Focus, FAQs and Factfile: Digitalvision.

Artwork credits

t = top; b = bottom; c = center; r = right; l = left

Richard Bonson: 78b; John Francis (Bernard Thornton Artists): 15cr. Paul Guest: 81c. Jacey: 5–7. Rob Jakeway: 68–69; 79b; 80t. Martin Sanders: 15t; 16–17c; 27br; 32bl; 40b; 43tb; 45t; 60b; 70–71. Peter Sarson: 81t. Steve Woosnam-Savage: 9c; 30–31c; 49b. Peter David Scott (Wildlife Art): 35c. Guy Smith: 11t & b;12b; 20–21; 22b; 23t; 24b; 38tr; 40t; 45c; 62b; 65–66; 74l; 75c & b; 79t & c. Roger Stewart 78c. Michael White: 12–13c; 14–15c; 34–35c; 36–37; 48b.